William Golding's Lord of the Flies
adapted for the stage by Nigel Williams

Lord of the Flies appeared in 1954. It was William
Golding's first published novel, and years later he said that
writing the book was "like lamenting the lost childhood of
the world". Golding who was born in 1911 and served in
the Royal Navy during the Second World War, worked for
many years as a schoolmaster. He went on to produce
another eleven novels, among them *The Inheritors,
Pincher Martin, The Spire,* and *Darkness Visible.* He won
the Booker Prize in 1980 with *Rites of Passage.* Golding
was awarded the Nobel Prize for Literature in 1983 and
was knighted in 1988. He died in 1993.

Nigel Williams was born in Cheshire in 1948, educated at
Highgate School and Oriel College, Oxford and is married
with three sons. He is the author of TV and stage plays,
and several novels, including the bestselling *Wimbledon
Poisoner, They Came from* SW19, *East of Wimbledon* and
Scenes from a Poisoner's Life.

William Golding's
Lord of the Flies

adapted for the stage by
Nigel Williams

faber and faber

First published in Great Britain in 1996
by Faber and Faber Limited
Bloomsbury House
74–77 Great Russell Street
London WC1B 3DA

Photoset by Parker Typesetting Service, Leicester
Printed and bound by CPI Group (UK) Ltd, Croydon, CR0 4YY

© Nigel Williams 1996

*All rights whatsoever in this play are strictly reserved and applications to
perform it should be made in writing, before rehearsals begin, to
Simpson Fox, 52 Shaftesbury Avenue, London W1V 7DE.
No performance may be given without a licence being obtained.*

A CIP catalogue record for this book
is available from the British Library
ISBN 978-0-571-16056-3

15 17 19 18 16

Contents

Story master

'And did you enjoy being little savages?' said Sir William Golding to the cast of the King's School Wimbledon production of *Lord of the Flies*.

'Ye-eahh!' they said.

'Ah!' said Sir William, 'but I don't think you'd enjoy being little savages all the time, would you?'

The thirty or forty small boys looked at him. This was the autumn of 1992 and Bill had been forty years out of teaching. He was a Nobel prizewinner. He had written what many (including me) think the greatest novel in English since the Second World War. But he was still a schoolmaster and the kids knew class when they saw it.

'Er . . . no, sir . . .' said one of them.

Bill grinned then.

'Well done!' he said.

There were many pleasurable things about adapting *Lord of the Flies* for the stage, but the greatest pleasure was seeing my stage version performed at my sons' school in Wimbledon, and having the performance witnessed by a man I only learned to call Bill a few short months before he died.

William Golding, as Ted Hughes pointed out at his memorial service, was a novelist whose work has a Shakespearian grandeur, and the high seriousness of his tragic vision is something you rarely find in contemporary fiction. In adapting his work for the stage I was forced, not to invent exactly, but to find a language that matched the violence and the drama of his imagination. It is *King Lear* rather than Nigel Williams or Stephen Poliakoff.

And, these days, where else to do a serious play but in a school?

'Would you like to sign the visitors' book?' said Colin Holloway, the headmaster. (I have always been a little frightened of Colin Holloway. He is a serious character and, as my own father was a headmaster, I am always a little overimpressed by the profession.)

'Of course!' said Bill.

With his white sailor's beard, canny expression and solid, physical grace, he didn't look at all like an author. He looked as if he had just come back from a round-the-world sailing trip. He had a peasant simplicity too – the aspect of a man who lives off the land and knows the value of things.

Bill Golding was, in spite of his great fame, not an arrogant man. He was, in my brief experience of him, interested in people, not as fans or material, but because he thought of himself, not as a guru or a celebrity, but as one of them. He went through to the headmaster's office and dutifully signed the visitors' book.

I still didn't know what he thought of the show. He had sat next to me in the King's Wimbledon Hall while Alan Dennis's production went on and he had listened patiently while I had told him that the King's College Junior School English master was five times as intelligent and theatrically skilled as your average Royal National Theatre director, but he hadn't yet said what he thought of it.

I was a little worried about what, down in Wimbledon, we still call the scenery.

One of my main aims in adapting the novel was to try to realize the complexity of his intentions. The way in which Golding uses myth and naturalism calls for the kind of seriousness of theatrical language that has all but vanished from our stages. When it appears it is usually howled down as pretentious or cried up as significant. What Golding's book has is a real knowledge of its subject – schoolboys – and a real conviction that they can represent more than the things they seem. They are animated by an important debate about power, democracy and the good or evil that is within men's hearts, but they are also, all too vividly, real boys of the kind you might find in any prep school today, forty years after the book was written.

He once said to me that one of the main aims of his book was to tell the story of the breakdown of English parliamentary democracy. 'Don't make them into little Americans, will you,' he added.

As we worked on the show Bill had been as sweet and generous as only a good teacher can be about the language I had chosen for our children ('I think the way you make them talk is amazing,' he wrote to me once) but the final test – whether the thing actually worked when you sat in a darkened room watching it with a few hundred Wimbledonians – had not yet been passed.

When Bill had signed the visitors' book, we all went out into the playground. His wife Ann Golding, who had said to me in Brown's Hotel, a week earlier: 'Mind how you go on that bicycle, we are getting rather fond of you,' was looking studied and neutral. Had she hated it? Or was it just that, in a long and extremely interesting life she had just seen too many young men drop off the perch. (She had told me, the first time we met, that one of the first people she walked out with had died in the Spanish Civil War.) Bill had spent much of the second act with his head in his hands. I was far too frightened to ask him what he thought of the proceedings. In fact, by now, I assumed that my version of his masterpiece had taken the same route to hell as the two film versions, of which he, purportedly, disapproved.

Instead I joined my wife as the Golding party headed

towards the car park. Was it, perhaps, my son? Had Jack screwed it up? Should I have cast him as Simon? Was the thing unstageable? Was it the stage itself (put together, the night before, by the King's College Wimbledon stage crew, a hardened body of men that I think included Mr Ned Williams, my eldest son)? Should we have done something more elaborate than a papier mâché pig? Was a red reflector, a torch and some silver paper really enough to give the impression of a bonfire big enough to roast a pig? Had Nugent remembered his line?

As the party walked away from the school, Matthew walked back to me. He had the airy, casual stance of the born negotiator. He was drawing deeply on a cigarette. I looked, nervously, back towards Bill and his wife, who were deep in conversation.

'What does he think?' I said.

Matthew grinned.

'Basically,' he said, 'he thinks it's OK.'

I am forty-seven years old. I have written ten or fifteen plays, many of which have been performed all over the world. I have stood up in the Théâtre National Populaire and had a whole theatre applaud me – perhaps under the mistaken impression that I was Howard Barker. I have been fashionable and unfashionable. I have been praised by Michael Coveney and slated by Benedict Nightingale. And, frankly, my dear, I don't give a damn any more. But I have never known an excitement as pure and simple as I had that night. It was my boys' school. It was my adaptation. But (and this is the most important thing) I had received the approbation of a writer whom I have admired since I was twelve, a writer who started me out writing, a writer who I wish was still here to praise or blame what I have done to his masterpiece, a great Englishman – Sir William Golding.

The play thanks to Adrian Noble and Elijah Moshinsky

was performed at the Royal Shakespeare Theatre in Stratford, summer of 1995. But, sadly, Bill was not there to see it.

Nigel Williams
1995

The first production of this adaption of **Lord of the Flies** was performed by King's College Junior School, Wimbledon, on 3 December 1991. The cast was as follows:

Ralph Richard South
Jack Luke Escombe
Piggy Christopher Melville
Roger David Pirrie
Sam Edward Maxwell
Eric Luke Toyne
Simon Jack Williams
Henry Max Berendt
Maurice David Galsworthy
Bill Leo Abrahams
Perceval Philip Jockelson
Peter Peter Cureton
Roberts Neil Roberts
Naval Officer Alan Dennis

Directed by Alan Dennis

The first professional production of this adaption of **Lord of the Flies** was first performed by the Royal Shakespeare Company at The Other Place, Stratford-upon-Avon, on 31 July 1995. The cast was as follows:

Ralph Daniel Brocklebank
Jack Mark Elliot
Piggy Christopher Hudson
Roger Tom McKay
Sam Tom Jones-Berney
Eric Edward Wilson
Simon Edmund Kingsley
Henry Benjamin Beeston
Maurice Matthew Wright
Bill Matthew Bannister
Perceval Dominic Skinner
Naval Officer Anthony Hannan
Naval Officer Christopher Middleton

Directed by Elijah Moshinsky
Designed by Chris Dyer

Act One

The lights go up on an almost bare raked stage, rising up to a cyclorama that, for the moment anyway, delineates the back area in which the action is played. Everything looks blue, as faraway as the eye can see. Brilliant white light on opening. No one on stage, and then **Ralph,** *a boy aged between twelve and thirteen wearing an English public school uniform, enters from the left, blinking up at the sun. As he stands there* **Piggy,** *a short plump boy of about his age, not in uniform, comes in behind him.*

Ralph It's amazing!

Piggy What's amazin'?

Ralph The sun.

Piggy sits, unimpressed.

Piggy Don't see what's so amazin'.

Ralph It's like a huge eye looking down at you.

Piggy It's hot. That's what it is. Hot.

Ralph turns and notices him for the first time.

Ralph That's a funny T-shirt.

Piggy My auntie give it me.

Pause.

It's a jersey anyway.

Ralph starts to strip to his underwear.

Ralph So? (*And stands facing the sun.*) It's amazing!

I

But Piggy stays huddled up into himself.

Ralph That's a lagoon. Great for swimming.

Piggy Can't swim.

Ralph Can't you?

Piggy I sink.

Ralph laughs.

Ralph You don't you know.

Piggy I do. I know I do.

Ralph pulls at Piggy's stomach.

Ralph (*quite amiable*) Blubber . . .

Piggy Leave off.

Pause.

What's your name?

Ralph Ralph. What's yours?

Piggy Not telling.

Ralph Is it a secret?

Piggy It's a stupid name.

Ralph What is it?

Piggy Are they all dead do you think?

Ralph What?

Piggy The plane broke up. It's in two bits.

Ralph They can't be.

Piggy Why not? (*Sitting up.*) If they weren't they'd be here. Organizin'. And worse things happen. My auntie says –

2

Ralph What does your auntie say?

Piggy A lot.

The two boys grin.

My head really hurts.

Ralph I'm sorry.

Piggy That's why I can't swim.

Ralph Why?

Piggy Assma.

Ralph 'Assma'?

Piggy Asthma. I get it. (*He's almost proud of this.*) Quite badly in fact.

Ralph Do you?

Piggy Quite badly.

Pause.

Maybe they're all dead anyway.

Ralph What?

Piggy Here. There. Everywhere. All over.

Ralph Don't be stupid. (*This idea frightens him.*)

Piggy Could be.

Pause.

They got bombs now . . . could . . .

Ralph They're not all dead, stupid. Not everyone in England, stupid. Not the whole of the British Isles. Not our parents. (*He moves centre stage and does a handstand.*)

Piggy Could be. That's good!

Ralph It's easy. You just have to –

He does it again. Piggy full of admiration.

Piggy Thass good!

Ralph You try!

Piggy Can't.

Ralph Come on. If you know so much . . .

Piggy Can't.

Ralph Give us your feet. I'll pull you . . .

Piggy Oh blimey.

Piggy submits to having his feet pulled. Making feeble attempts to get his hands on the ground. Ralph pulls him round so that he is standing on his head.

Ralph What's your name?

Piggy What?

Ralph What's your name?

Piggy Piggy.

Ralph lets go.

Ralph Piggy?

Piggy Piggy.

Ralph Amazing.

Piggy But you're not to tell anyone. Not anyone.

Ralph I won't. Piggee! Piggee!

Piggy Don't!

Ralph Sorry.

4

Pause.

I won't then.

Pause.

I'm Ralph.

*He has spotted something. Down front. It is the conch,
a creamy white horn-shaped shell.*

Look!

Piggy Look where?

Ralph Look at this!

Piggy What is it?

Ralph It's a shell. (*Holding it.*) A conch. That's what they
call it. A conch.

Piggy I seen one. At my auntie's friend's house. I –

Ralph You blow in them, don't you?

Piggy I don't.

Ralph You blow in them and they make a noise.

Piggy I don't. My assma . . .

Ralph From down here. (*Indicates his diaphragm.*) It's
like the flute. I'm in the orchestra.

Piggy You what?

Ralph The flute. You know. Not the flute. The saxophone.
Or the clarinet.

Piggy Uh?

Ralph Don't you know anything? It makes a noise . . .

He spits and blows. A fantastic farting sound comes out.

Piggy Oh what?

Both boys fall about laughing.

Do it again then. Since you're in the orchestra.

And another farting noise.

Some orchestra!

Ralph You can, though! You can make a really good noise. If you get it right.

Piggy Yeah?

One more farting sound. Much laughter.

Ralph I bet there are people. I bet there are some others here. And I bet if I blow I'll call them. They'll come. I bet. And –

Piggy And what?

Ralph I don't know what.

Pause.

Piggy Call 'em then. If they're there less call 'em. Eh? Blow. And let 'em all come.

And Ralph blows again. This time a long and sweet note echoes across the stage. A pause and then it is answered by a boy's soprano on the same note. Ralph plays again. And another note. Piggy has moved upstage pointing off right.

Look! Over there!

*And once more a note is sounded and answered, nearer this time. And again. And then the note is picked up by other voices. A real professional chord sound. Louder and louder. And then at the height of the dialogue between the boys' voices and the conch, **Jack Merridew***

*and the choir are on the stage in full choir school drag.
Jack is walking back, urging them on. In a line behind
him are* **Simon, Sam, Eric,** *and* **Henry,** *straggling a little.*

Jack Where's the man with the trumpet? In a line! Come
on! In a line!

But the line breaks up as they come on.

You have to keep in a line! Otherwise . . .

Simon Otherwise what, Merridew?

Jack Otherwise . . .

Pause.

You have to keep line. That's all.

Simon I'm hot.

Jack Who was blowing the trumpet?

Ralph Me.

*Jack and Ralph face each other. Ralph anxious to get
on. Jack quite impassive.*

You're the choir.

Jack Yes.

Ralph You're good.

Jack I thought it was a grown-up. I got them to sing.

Ralph You're good.

Jack I'm choir prefect. The others are slacking. (*and to his
lot*) And so are you. (*Crossing up right, shouting.*) Come on!

Ralph I'm Ralph.

Jack Merridew. (*Pointing to Simon.*) That's Cambourne.
That's –

7

Sam Sam –

Eric 'N Eric –

Jack They're all slack beasts. Are we going to have proper names or what? Like school? I –

Piggy I'll take 'em down.

Jack Who's he?

Ralph He's . . .

Pause.

I don't know who he is.

Piggy I'll take names. (*Crossing to Simon.*) What was you?

Jack We have to have some system you see. (*Crossing up right again. Shouts.*) Come on then!

Ralph Look! Over there! By those trees! There are some little kids. D'you see?

Jack But no grown-ups!

Ralph They were in the front of the plane. They –

Jack (*shouts*) Come on you! You too! Juniors or whatever you are! Come on! (*with amazement*) Why is he just lying on the beach?

Ralph Well . . .

Jack Well what?

Ralph I s'pose he can . . .

Jack Can what?

Ralph Well . . .

Pause.

He's got all day.

8

Jack All day to do what? That's the question! (*Going up right again. Calling*) Come on then!

And in bedraggled choir uniforms come **Maurice** *and* **Bill.**

Why can't you keep in line?

Maurice It's hot, Merridew.

Jack (*to Ralph as much as to anyone*) I'm choir prefect. What are you?

Ralph I'm . . . (*A grin.*) I'm Ralph. I dunno.

Piggy We should have a meetin'.

Jack Should we? (*Doesn't like the sound of this kid.*) Who did you say he was?

Ralph Ask him.

Piggy All I said was – we should 'ave a meetin'.

Jack Who are you?

Piggy Never mind who I am. (*to Simon*) We should 'ave a meetin'. (*He stops.*) An' we should take all the names and get organized.

Jack Well, we'll start with your name shall we?

Piggy All I'm saying is –

Ralph He's got quite a funny name in fact . . .

Piggy Ralph!

Ralph What?

Piggy You promised.

Ralph Promised what?

Piggy You know what.

Ralph I don't know what you're on about.

Piggy You know – you –

Ralph His name's Piggy, in fact.

Jack Piggy?

Piggy You promised!

Piggy's wetness irritating Ralph.

Ralph Piggy!

Jack and Ralph drawing together.

Jack Oh! Too perfect!

Piggy (*shouts*) You promised!

Ralph (*shouts*) I never!

Piggy (*shouts*) You did! You promised!

Ralph (*shouts*) Well you were being stupid!

Maurice Why do we want a meeting? What do we want a meeting for?

Ralph Because . . . (*He looks from Jack to Piggy.*)

Piggy To see about being rescued. An' we have to have a meetin'. To decide.

Jack First of all we have to decide who's in charge. And I should be in charge because I'm a prefect. (*to Ralph*) Are you a prefect in your school?

Ralph I will be. Probably.

Jack Where are you?

Ralph Upton.

Jack I don't know that. Is that a good school?

Ralph It's OK I suppose.

Aware they have got off the track, Piggy gets back to his point.

Piggy I go to Barnabas High. Anyone know it?

Jack No, 'Piggy', in fact we don't, 'Piggy', and if that's its uniform I don't think we do want to know it do we?

Simon He's right though. We should. We should have a meeting.

Jack turns on him.

Jack Cambourne has spoken! We have to have a meeting! Well done, Cambourne!

Ralph What did you say your name was?

Simon Simon.

Jack Cambourne.

Simon Simon Cambourne.

Jack It has to be names like at school doesn't it? Otherwise we'll all end up like a lot of savages.

Maurice and Bill do gorilla impressions. Much 'hoo hooing'. The lads all enjoy this. But Jack has moved up right and is looking off.

(*shouts*) Come on you lot! Come on! (*He turns back on the others.*)

Ralph He's right really.

Jack Who is?

Ralph Him. Piggy. He's right really. We have to have a meeting.

Jack Meetings are jolly useful of course.

Ralph Where do you say you were at . . . ?

Jack Godstone.

Ralph Oh yes.

Jack Have you heard of it?

Ralph I think so.

Maurice steps forward. Big, amiable, not bright.

Maurice We thrashed Audley House at rugger.

Bill We completely annihilated them.

Simon They did. It was quite horrible.

Ralph My dad says if you can run with the ball . . .

Jack Where do you play? Are you useful?

Ralph I'm a forward. (*He has the conch in his hands.*) I can run with the ball. I . . .

Jack is running for him.

(*shouts*) Hey!

Ralph passes it to Maurice who runs with him. Jack goes for Maurice. Although he's small he's a fierce tackler. Maurice passes it to Bill who passes it back to Ralph, who is tackled by Jack and Jack brings him down. As he falls down Ralph throws the conch to Piggy, who catches it. Ralph and Jack's tackle brings the game to a halt since their sort of rivalry is, at the moment anyway, the kind that might be sanctioned by either of their schools.

Jack Not bad! You're not bad!

Both are lying down.

Ralph Well . . . you know . . . only a genius . . .

Piggy When you've all finished runnin' all over the place, maybe we can start doin' things prop'ly because if all the grown-ups aren't here I mean if there aren't any I mean if the bombs have . . .

This scares Jack into violence.

Jack (*shouts*) Shut up, can't you? You stupid little boy!

Pause.

Ralph Who's going to be in charge? Will it be one person or –

Simon You have to have a vote.

Piggy You do. You have to have a vote.

Sam And you have to –

Eric Count up the –

Sam Numbers and then –

Eric If you're on your –

Sam Feet.

Pause.

You talk.

Ralph We can't all talk at once.

Sam I know that's what –

Eric We're –

Sam Saying, we –

Eric Always talk –

Sam Together and it gets –

Eric Confusing.

13

Pause.

Ralph We might you know.

Maurice Might what?

Ralph Might have to have rules. If what Piggy . . . if what he . . . says is right then . . . maybe there is, you know . . . just us . . .

Jack Is that so bad?

Simon Depends on us.

Jack So what? So what if they're all dead. Eh? (*Striding round.*) Look. Look over there. There's fruit on those trees. And there's fish in the sea. And it'll be like . . . it doesn't matter. We can do whatever we like can't we?

Bill (*shouts*) Ye-eaahh!

Maurice Smash the place up . . .

Henry (*shouts*) Ye-eeaah!

Maurice Midnight feasts! (*He does his gorilla impression. This last remark is, of course, intended to be satirical.*)

Bill (*shouts*) Murder unlimited!

Piggy We can't, though. We can't. We can't do jus' as we like. An' if we all talk at the same time we'll never get nowhere will we? I'll tell you what. I'll tell you what . . . (*He still has the conch left over from the rugger game. He holds it up. Very earnest*) This shell. This shell thingy . . . If we're in a meetin' 'ooever holds the shell means that person is talkin'. And that is a rule. A rule, you hear me? An' it must never be broken.

The intellectual daring of this silences even Jack.

Ralph (*quietly*) OK.

Jack Just because he says.

Ralph Well . . .

Jack Is it a rule just because he says?

Ralph Well . . . it . . .

Simon The question is . . . Is it a good rule?

Ralph You what?

Simon Is it good? That's all.

Ralph You're funny.

Jack He is. He's weird. He's a Buddha man he's . . .

Simon From another planet.

Jack I think we should talk about the leader and who's the leader because you always need a leader and –

Piggy You can't.

Jack Can't what?

Piggy Can't talk.

Jack Can't what?

Piggy You 'aven't got the shell. I got the shell.

Jack Look –

Maurice Is it a rule though?

Bill It's a roo-ool!

Sam School rules –

Eric Must be obeyed and –

Sam At all times boys must –

Eric Wear a cap on the premises and –

Jack (*shouts*) OK it's a rule. (*to Piggy*) Give me the shell. And I'll say something.

Piggy I 'aven't said what I was goin' ter say.

Jack Well say it and we'll all yawn and then pass me the shell.

Piggy All I was sayin' was . . . (*Now he has the floor he is a little tongue-tied.*) We don't know 'ow many's on the island. We don't know. We 'ave to get them all together an' 'ave a meetin'.

Jack Right. Pass me the shell then.

> *A tense pause. Piggy looks at Ralph, but no help forthcoming there. He passes it to Maurice, who passes it to Bill and so on round the group until it reaches Jack. Jack likes the power of it.*

Now. I'm talking. And I have the shell. And I think . . . (*looking round*) I think I should be leader. Because I'm choir prefect.

Piggy Why?

Jack Because. Because it's a good idea, stupid. Anyway you can't speak. I've got the shell.

Maurice My turn for the shell.

Piggy You mustn't –

Jack Catch me, Walsh! You wish . . .

Maurice First to get it . . .

Jack Come on then! Come on then! (*He starts to feint. A small kid but with the rather admirable aggression of the natural games player.*)

Bill To me! To me!

Jack Come on, Walsh! Come on then . . .

Maurice lunges. Jack dodges and passes the shell to Bill.

Piggy (*shouts*) No! This ain't proper! This ain't –

Ralph This ain't cricket, Piggy!

He moves out, watching to see where the shell will go. Maurice has headed for Bill and Bill passes to Henry. Simon is merely watching.

Jack (*calls loudly for it from Henry*) To me! To me!

But just as Henry is about to pass, Ralph does a very neat tackle. They fall and Ralph ends up with the shell, waving it like a trophy.

Ralph (*shouts triumphantly*) It's mine! It's mine! It's mine! (*He stays very still, holding the conch aloft. The light catches it.*)

Piggy Ralph! Ralph for leader!

This is said, of course, because of his hostility to Jack. But Ralph's stillness and the fact that he is holding the conch aloft make the others pick up the cry.

Jack If you want me for leader . . .

Ralph If you want Jack for leader. Put up your hands!

Sam Ralph –

Eric For leader! Ralph!

Ralph Put up your hands! If you want me for leader!

And all, apart from Jack, put up their hands. Jack is mortified.

Jack If you want me for leader I said. If you want me, then you have to put up your hands. If you don't want to be stupid. If you want to be . . .

As he is speaking, **Roger,** *a small, insignificant-looking boy, comes from the back.*

If you want to follow . . . you know . . . people are so pathetic! Look at him! (*He means Piggy.*)

At the back, with curious, almost sinister quietness, Roger puts up his hands. He is smiling.

If you want firm leadership, in fact if you know what that is – people slacking, people not pulling their weight, go on put your hands up.

Ralph Who are you?

Roger Roger.

Ralph You're a bit late I'm afraid. We've already got a leader.

Roger Who's that?

Ralph Me. (*to Jack*) But you must have the choir of course. They're yours.

Maurice They could be an army.

Henry If we're attacked . . .

Bill Or hunters . . .

Sam They could do, if we –

Eric Got attacked by –

Sam Strangers.

Roger has moved downstage.

Simon What school are you from?

Roger Does it matter?

Simon Well, it might, I suppose.

Roger I'm from nowhere school. That's where I'm from.

Simon I thought I'd seen you before.

Jack In a dream, did you, Cambourne? Was it in one of your dreams?

Simon What's wrong with me, Merridew? What's –

Jack 'What's wrong with me?' Everything.

Ralph Listen.

Jack 'Ralph for leader.'

Ralph Listen – (*He still has the shell. He holds it up aloft.*) I'm leader. And there's no need for fighting. Because we're all one gang. One gang. And this is our island. It belongs to all of us. Doesn't it?

Piggy Unless there's natives . . .

Jack If there were natives they would have been here by now . . .

Ralph It's ours. All ours. I'm sure of it. It looks like that, don't you think? Look at it. Sand. Blue sea. Those palms. Look at it. There's no one. No one but us.

Jack responds to this.

Jack Look up there – there's a great hill . . .

Ralph Do as a look-out! (*He means the top end of the raked stage.*)

Piggy Hang on!

Ralph Hang on where?

Piggy Ralph, you're leader – it's a meetin' thass what it's –

Jack It's an adventure, stupid!

Piggy Ralph's got the conch, 'e –

Jack Ralph, it's amazing up here . . . (*He has started to move up the rake.*) It's amazing. You can see right across the island!

Piggy (*shouts*) It's a meetin'!

Jack Ralph, it's really good.

Piggy Ralph, you can talk. You got the conch. You talk.

Ralph can't resist Jack.

Ralph You talk, Piggy. (*Tosses him the shell.*) Talk about your auntie. Talk to yourself.

Roger Talk rubbish.

Jack (*shouts*) Come on!

One by one the boys are drifting up to the crest of the stage.

Sam Look over there, it's –

Eric All blue, you can –

Sam See right round the –

Eric Island!

Henry Look at those trees!

Bill Brilliant! Brilliant, wonderful, it's all blue.

Ralph has joined them.

Ralph (*shouts*) Our island!

Jack (*shouts*) Treasure island!

Bill (*shouts*) Coral island!

Henry (*shouts*) Castaways!

Jack (*shouts*) Three cheers for our island! Hip-Hip –

Piggy (*shouts*) Lissen!

All (*shouting*) Hooray!

Jack (*shouts*) Hip-hip –

All (*shouting*) Hooray!

Jack (*shouts*) Hip-hip –

All (*shouting*) Hooray!

Simon is halfway between Piggy and the others. He is really, animally, excited.

Jack (*shouts*) Look! Look!

Ralph It's a pig!

Simon Look at it go!

Sam Where?

Simon There! There!

Eric I can't see it . . .

They are crowding round Jack, looking out to the back of the stage.

Jack It came out of those trees. It was running with its head down. It's come back. You see? (*He's very excited.*) It's come back! There it goes! See?

Simon It's amazing! Look at it!

Sam Let's get it! Come on! Let's get it!

Ralph Steady on . . .

Jack Steady on what?

Ralph One thing at a time!

Jack What thing at a time?

Ralph How would you get it?

Jack Get sticks of course . . .

Eric We haven't got sticks!

Piggy is down at the front of the stage. A long way from them.

Piggy (*calls*) What are you doing?

Jack I've been hunting. In England. I've been hunting. It's good fun. I've been out with the hunters.

Pause.

When they blood you they put blood all over you. I'm a good hunter in fact. I'm a natural hunter. We should sharpen sticks and go hunting. We should . . .

Ralph What we need . . . what we need . . .

Maurice Is a good shit!

All laugh. Maurice the clown.

Ralph What we need is a fire.

Silence.

We need to build a fire. Up here. Where it can be seen. And there needs to be smoke from the fire. And then a ship will see it. And rescue us.

This idea has got their attention.

My dad's in the Navy. And he says the Queen has this room. And in this room is a map, with absolutely all the islands in the world on it. And when they realize the plane has gone missing, they'll send out ships and look. And they'll look and look and look until they find us.

Roger Will they?

Ralph They will. And that's why the fire has to be –

Roger If there's any of them left.

Ralph They –

Roger They'll bomb each other to bits, won't they? Isn't that why we were sent away like that? To get away from the bombs? Well . . .

Pause.

They get bigger and bigger bombs. There won't be any of them left, will there? There probably isn't a Queen left. Or any of those things. Just us. (*Throwing earth.*) Why should they? Why should they bother to follow us? They're all too busy . . . (*He does that frightening mime again.*) killing one another.

Ralph Listen –

Jack To what?

Ralph You voted me chief. Right?

Pause.

We'll make a fire.

This makes some impact on them.

Jack And how will we start it?

Maurice With sticks. Like de native!

Bill No no you rub them together –

This stops them short. Piggy is now alone at the down front area of the stage. He calls up.

Ralph Glasses!

Jack Whose glasses?

Ralph Piggy's glasses! Him! Down there! Piggy!

Jack Thought we'd find a use for him . . .

Maurice Don't want you, you know but . . .

Roger Just love your glasses!

Ralph Piggy's glasses!

Simon You can you know. Because the sun's rays . . .

Jack 'The sun's rays' . . . what, Professor Cambourne?

But Ralph is calling down to Piggy.

Ralph (*shouts*) Piggy!

Roger Look at them.

Jack Look at who?

Roger Those two. (*He throws a stone.*) They love each other.

Maurice Let's keep a watch!

Jack For what?

Maurice For pig. Keep a watch.

Bill Yeah! And when the time comes . . .

Jack Yeah!

Ralph Come on. It isn't just kid's stuff. It's serious. Come on. I'm chief right? So listen. We should get rescued, OK? So Piggy, let's have your glasses.

Piggy You what?

Jack 'You what?'

Piggy Is that what you was after?

Ralph Listen –

Piggy I need my glasses.

Jack What do you need glasses for then?

24

Piggy See with, a' course.

Jack 'To see with.' Brilliant.

Ralph Piggy – we need your glasses.

Piggy You can't! You rush off in the middle of a meetin' and –

Roger Shut up and give him the glasses.

Piggy I won't!

Jack Give him the glasses or we'll make you.

Piggy I don't see why I should.

Roger Shut up and give him the glasses.

Piggy Ralph –

But Ralph doesn't respond to this appeal.

I mean . . . be fair . . . I mean . . . (*he takes them off, muttering*) Don't see why I should . . .

Jack Thank you . . .

Piggy Can't see nothing now!

Jack So kind of you.

Piggy Jus' a blur . . .

Ralph Get leaves!

Piggy Can't see a thing . . .

Jack And twigs!

Ralph That's it! Leaves and twigs!

Jack Look at that sun!

Ralph It'll catch. You'll see. It'll catch!

Jack and Ralph are co-conspirators in this. Piggy

25

watches, excluded. The others are in a circle round them, respectful.

Simon It narrows the rays, you see.

Maurice Does it?

Simon To a point. We did it in science.

Ralph It is catching!

Jack It is!

Bill Like in –

Sam Stone –

Eric Age –

Sam Times!

Ralph It must have been like that.

Jack I bet.

Ralph You made fire . . .

Jack And you hunted . . .

Ralph And you . . .

Piggy is really lost without his glasses. He moves into the group nonetheless.

Piggy Excuse me.

Ralph What?

Piggy I can't see nothing.

They carry on in the routine of the fire ritual.

And what do you mean 'stone-age times'? Stone-age times? Are these stone-age times? I 'adn't noticed. And did stone-age people have glasses I'd like to know. I don't think so. Or if they did – did they grab them off of each

26

other? Those are my glasses. (*with contempt*) You're just a pack of kids. You can't just make a fire an' not think about it. You got to do it carefully and prop'ly. You –

Ralph It's catching!

Jack It is. It's catching!

Maurice Look at that go!

Piggy I want my glasses!

Jack turns on him.

Jack Shut up can't you? I don't know who you are or what you're doing here but just shut up can't you?

Piggy Ralph – you tell 'im – you –

But Ralph is quite absorbed in the fire.

Ralph Look at that! Look at that go!

Bill It's spreading!

Henry Isn't it just?

Piggy Yes, it is innit? It's goin' mad. An' if you don't build a fire prop'ly it does go mad. In fact if –

Simon Look, it'll get out of control . . .

Ralph He's right . . .

Jack So what if it gets out of control? So what?

Ralph Look it's spreading . . . Oh, for God's sake . . .

Simon It is . . . it's . . .

And indeed smoke is billowing out wildly. They haven't set out a barrier for the fire and so it is spreading too fast across the back of the stage. We see a line of smoke, really getting out of control.

Bill It's out of control.

Sam It's a forest –

Eric Fire!

Maurice Water . . .

Piggy Water? Water? Wocher mean water? Yes, iss out a' control in case you 'adn't noticed!

Roger So what if it's out of control? What's it to you if it's out of control?

Ralph (*shouts*) Stamp it out!

Roger Listen –

Ralph Jack, we ought to! We ought to stamp it out!

Jack is not sure whether to agree with this, but there is a sense in which he can make deals with Ralph . . .

Jack Yes!

Bill Yes!

Henry Stamp it out!

Ralph Stamp it out everyone!

Jack It's catching on the grass!

Maurice Hey! Forest fire!

Piggy (*shouts*) Yeah! Forest fire! Yeah! If you'd a listened to me. You'd a not bin in this mess wouldjer? Forest fire!

Ralph (*shouts*) Shut up, Piggy and stamp!

Jack (*shouts*) Yes stamp! Stamp everyone!

Maurice (*shouts*) We stamp de fire!

Bill (*shouts*) Stamping dance!

Henry (*shouts*) Stamp those feet!

Maurice (*shouts*) Get de rhydmn!

All the boys are now stamping across the back of the stage. All, that is, apart from Piggy. Ralph, annoyed with himself for his mistake, screams at him.

Ralph (*shouts*) Don't stand there like a great fat, wet weed! Stamp! Stamp, can't you?

Piggy (*shouts*) Why should I? Iss you goes out when there's a meeting and does things stupid and takes my glasses, why should I? Why should I stamp when I can't even see my glasses?

But the boys are quite abandoned to this new game.

Jack (*shouts*) Stamp!

Boys (*shouting*) Stamp!

Jack (*shouts*) We stamp!

Boys (*shouting*) We stamp!

Ralph (*shouts*) It's going! We've got it! It's stopping!

Jack (*shouts*) Stamp!

Boys (*shouting*) Stamp!

Jack (*shouts*) We stamp!

Boys (*shouting*) We stamp!

The smoke starts to die down. Sudden peace.

Ralph We did it!

Piggy Did what? What didjer do? What?

Ralph Look!

The smoke has billowed down across the stage and, as it

clears, in the middle, alone, down front, is revealed the
small figure of **Perceval Wemys Madyson**. *A lit'lun of*
around six or seven. The boys look down on him as if
he were a visitor from Mars which, in his neat school
uniform, his shining satchel and perfect prep school
gear, he could well be.

It's a little kid!

Jack Must have seen the smoke!

Piggy And what you goin' ter do about him, eh? Woch
you goin' ter do about him an' all the other lit'luns?
There's a load of 'em over there isn't there?

Simon I don't know.

Jack Cambourne.

Simon I don't know what we know.

Pause.

I don't know where we are or what this island is or
whether it's a good island. It looks like a good island but is
it? I don't know.

Jack turns on him.

Jack You are always saying things to be clever,
Cambourne, and to make people feel scared or something.
Because you're a weirdie who froths at the mouth and falls
down in matins.

The choir laughs. Jack feels better about his status now.
And they follow him down. Ralph is talking to Perceval.

Perceval Was there a fire?

Ralph Yes. But it's gone.

Perceval Adam Jackson was next to me. But he isn't . . .

Ralph Isn't what?

Perceval Isn't here?

Ralph No.

Pause.

No.

Perceval I went into the trees . . .

Ralph Did you?

Perceval I did.

Ralph We should get you all together. It's all difficult.
We . . .

Perceval I saw something . . .

Ralph Did you? (*He's not really listening.*) Which school
are you from?

Perceval Not from your school.

Ralph We're from different schools.

Perceval Have the bombs killed everyone? Have they
killed our mums yet?

Ralph Listen –

Perceval We were sent because of the bombs, weren't we?

Ralph Yes. Now –

Perceval I am Perceval Wemys Madyson, The Vicarage,
Harcourt St Anthony.

The others are standing round him in a circle now.

Roger Good for you!

Perceval I went into the trees.

Ralph He's been in the trees he says.

Perceval And I saw something.

Jack What did you see?

Perceval A beastie.

Pause.

A snake thingy. I saw it.

Uneasy silence.

Jack Don't be stupid. There's no beastie. There –

Perceval I saw it. Over there. In the trees. I went in. And I saw this thing.

Ralph (*trying to comfort him, not quite sure of his ground*) I'm sure there isn't. I'm sure. We've been up to that hill. And you can see all around. It all looks . . . I'm sure there isn't. There's just us. No beast.

Jack He's being stupid.

Simon Unless . . .

Jack Unless what?

Simon Nothing . . .

Perceval There is a beast.

This is making them all nervous. Henry rounds on him.

Henry Why? Why is there a beast?

Perceval There just is.

Pause.

Because I saw it.

Simon has moved away from the group.

Simon The sun's going down. It's getting colder.

No one reacts to this.

Where do we sleep?

Ralph There can't be a beast.

Piggy Don't know about beasts. Know about animals. Know about snakes. But I dunno no beasts. All I know is I want my glasses. It's a meetin'. You got the shell.

Ralph (*shouts*) Shut up about your stupid meeting, can't you? And your shell and your glasses!

Piggy (*shouts*) Why should I?

Jack (*shouts*) Why should he give you your glasses? If he's chief, he can do anything with your glasses in fact! He can . . . (*groping for the word*) requisition them . . .

Roger He can do anything if he's a chief. That's what being a chief means.

Ralph (*to Perceval*) How far in the woods did you go?

Perceval Don't remember.

Jack We saw them from up there, Ralph. We saw the whole island.

Simon You have to go all over before you know. If it's a mountain you have to go to the top of the mountain and if it's a forest right to the heart of the forest.

Jack You use your eyes, Cambourne. That's all.

Pause.

If there is a beast we'll hunt it.

Ralph I just don't believe there is one. A beast, I mean. Look at it! Look at this island! Look over there – at the sand and the trees. And the sea, the way it comes in so

33

slowly. Out there . . . do you see . . . something jumped
. . . something blue . . . oh and . . . (*he stops.*)

Piggy Woss up?

Ralph There.

Jack Where?

Ralph On the horizon.

Bill Where? What?

Ralph Right over there. Do you see it?

Jack Where?

Ralph It is . . . I'm sure it is . . . Oh my (*screams*) God it
is . . .

Bill What's the –

Ralph (*shouts*) A ship! A ship!

Jack You what?

Ralph (*shouts*) There! There! A ship!

Maurice (*shouts*) Hey! (*Jumping up and down. Shouts*)
Hey!

Ralph (*shouts*) Don't be completely stupid! They can't
hear you!

Henry It is! It's a ship!

Sam I can see the –

Eric Smoke.

Henry Smoke . . .

Ralph Quick quick . . .

Jack Quick what?

Ralph The fire.

Jack What about it?

Ralph We need the fire . . .

Jack You're right!

Ralph The fire . . .

Piggy (*triumphant*) 'We need the fire!'

Ralph (*shouts*) Shut up! Shut up! Shut up! (*He still has Piggy's glasses. Looking round wildly*) Get rocks. We'll make a proper fire. Put the rocks round it. And keep it in so as it doesn't spread like last time. Get rocks. Come on.

Jack Get rocks. Come on you lot. Come on altos – get rocks.

Ralph (*shouts*) Come on back up the hill! Come on!

Piggy (*shouts*) 's all very well innit? 's all very well! 's a bit late though I reckon!

The boys are swarming back up the rake. Ralph with the glasses. Others scattering round the stage to find things to keep the fire in.

Henry Here's one!

Sam Here's –

Roger Another . . .

Ralph (*shouts*) Get leaves too!

Jack (*shouts*) Break those branches!

Bill Here's a rock.

Simon There's one here . . .

Ralph (*to Roger*) Come on, you!

35

Roger is simply standing, watching.

Roger It's too late!

Ralph Don't be stupid . . .

Roger It's moving the wrong way . . .

Ralph Don't be . . .

Henry Here's some more . . .

Ralph Trouble is . . .

Jack What's up?

Ralph The sun's lost strength . . .

Jack looking up.

Jack Come on! (*to the sky*) Come on God, you stupid!

Ralph Oh come on . . .

Sam More –

Eric Rocks here!

Bill Another one!

Henry Another one!

Ralph Oh come on, can't you?

Jack Try blowing on it . . .

Ralph It takes ages. That's the trouble.

Roger The ship's going!

Ralph Can't you do something useful?

Roger It's going!

Simon Blow on it!

Ralph I'm blowing!

Jack Blow harder!

Simon It's going!

Roger It's gone!

Jack It has Ralph!

Ralph Oh come on!

Simon (*shouts*) It's gone! Look! It's gone!

Ralph looks up from his position crouched over the fire.

Ralph It's gone.

Jack Yes.

Ralph It's gone.

Piggy (*shouts from below*) I toldjer didn't I? I toldjer not to be so stupid. I toldjer it was a meetin' an' that. An' we should a' done things in order. An' you wouldn't lissen wouldjer? (*Pause. Indicating Jack.*) When it comes to it you're all the same I reckon. Same lot you are. Look at you! Kneelin' over something thass no use now. Look at yerself.

Jack is waiting for Ralph to go for Piggy. But he doesn't. He gets up, slowly, glasses in hand.

Jack You going to let him talk to you like that?

Roger Chief.

Jack You going to let him? You going to let him talk to you like that?

Roger Chief?

Ralph Yes. (*He has finally realized what he's done. Crosses to Piggy with his glasses.*) I'm sorry.

Deathly silence as the others watch.

37

I'm sorry I took your glasses. I'm sorry I lost my temper.
I'm sorry I told them your name if it comes to that. I'm
sorry. You were right. If we hadn't . . . if the fire hadn't
. . . if we'd have thought. Piggy's right. We all got
carried away. We got stupid really. We must do things
prop'ly like he said. And this fire . . . now this fire is
started we must never let it out. There must always be
someone here to guard it and make sure it's kept, so that
if a ship comes and sees us we'll be rescued. Sam 'n' Eric
can start here. And we'll go down to the beach. And
build shelters. We have to start now. And be sensible.
That's what we have to do. And I say so. I'm chief and I
say so.

Jack Why do you listen to him? (*He sees this as a betrayal.
Looking for a way back to his audience.*) What's so great
about a fire anyway? What are we going to do with a fire
anyway? (*to the others*) We need sharp sticks, like spears,
to protect us.

Ralph Listen –

Jack No, you listen. You said I could have the choir, didn't
you? I thought you were a regular chap and you . . . suck
up to that . . . We need spears. That's what I'm saying. We
need a defence force. That's what I'm saying.

Ralph We need –

Jack We need it now. Before it gets dark. Before something
comes out of those trees . . .

Ralph This is a meeting. If you want to speak . . .

Jack Very well. I want to speak. I want to speak.

Piggy He –

Jack I want to speak.

Slowly, Ralph passes him the shell.

We must get spears. We must get weapons. It's getting dark. We don't know what's out there. But whatever it is, we're not afraid of it. Are we afraid of it?

All No.

Jack Are we afraid of it?

All (*shouting*) No!!

Jack Will we get spears?

All (*shouting*) Yes.

Roger (*shouts*) Get spears!

Maurice (*shouts*) Hunt de pig!

Boys (*shouting*) Hunt! Hunt! Hunt de pig!

> *Jack starts to lead them in a circle as they loudly chant, 'Hunt! Hunt! Hunt de pig!' The chant gets louder and louder.*

Ralph (*shouts*) Listen –

> *But they ignore him. The circle winds round until they reach the edge of the stage.*

(*screams*) I want to speak! Give me the conch!

> *The group stops. Jack pauses, then throws the shell across to Ralph.*

Jack You speak. And when we come back, we'll listen. We're not savages, you know. But we'll come back with spears.

Ralph I thought you . . .

Jack I thought you were quite a decent chap. Till you started crawling to that stupid fat little slug, who can't even speak properly. Sorry. 'Prop'ly.' Isn't that how it's pronounced these days. (*with the bitterness of betrayal*)

How could you? How could you say sorry to him? Just when you and I had a good gang. Just when we had a good gang. And as for meetings and doing things properly. Of course we'll do things properly.

Pause.

But there are limits you know.

Ralph I –

Jack has turned to the others.

Jack (*screams*) Hunt! Hunt! Hunt! Hunt! Kill de pig!

Boys (*screaming*) Yeah!

Jack (*screams*) Kill de pig!

Boys (*screaming*) Yeah!

Jack (*screams*) Hunt! Hunt! Hunt! Hunt!

And he leads them round and off towards the side of the stage. As they chant behind him, Ralph is left alone with Piggy, Simon, Sam, Eric and Perceval. He is holding the shell.

Ralph It's still a meeting. I . . .

Piggy Bunch a' kids.

Ralph What?

Piggy Bunch a' stupid kids . . .

Ralph What's so great about you, eh? What's so marvellous about you, fatso? (*He feels left out. Doesn't want to be with the wets and the weeds.*) If you hadn't . . .

Piggy I never done nothing.

Ralph Done anything. Can't you speak English? Done anything. You and your meetings. You and your . . . (*He* *goes to the edge of the stage.*) You go and talk to yourself in your meeting!

Piggy Don't leave us!

Ralph You're pathetic!

Piggy Am I?

Ralph Yes, you are. I'm going with them. I'm . . .

Piggy You can't!

Ralph Why can't I? Who made you chief I'd like to know. It's all your fault they ran off like that. You undermine my authority if you'd like to know. Why'd I have to stay here?

Piggy 'Cos you're chief. An' you know that. You're chief. An' they know that an' all. An' they'll be back. 'Course they will. They'll come back with their tails between their legs. 'Cos you're chief. An' you know what's right.

Very slowly Ralph turns and moves back to the centre of the stage.

Perceval Listen. I can hear the beastie.

Ralph That's not the beastie.

We hear the distant shouts of 'Hunt! Hunt! Hunt! Hunt!' Ralph turns towards it.

It's us.

Piggy It ain't us.

Simon Who is it then?

Piggy It's them.

Ralph looks back almost longingly at the distant sound.

Blackout.

Act Two

Darkness. The only real light source down front. The huge stage is otherwise all shadows. Some time has elapsed since the first passage of action but how much would be hard to judge since there is no way of keeping time. There has been time, anyway, to erect a tattered shelter down at the front of the stage. Asleep by it are Simon, Ralph, Piggy and Perceval, the lit'lun. Right up at the back, at the highest point of the raked stage, asleep by a dying fire, are Sam and Eric. The boys' clothes have deteriorated considerably since the last act. They are dressed in a bizarre parody of their school uniforms. Sam wakes up, suddenly, as if disturbed by some sound. He looks out to the very back of the stage, which is more darkness shrouded with a huge gauze.

Sam Eric –

Eric Sam –

Sam You're asleep . . .

Eric I'm not. Honest.

Sam You were.

Eric I wasn't. Honest.

Pause.

Sam Put some wood on it.

Eric I was going to.

Sam You were asleep.

43

Eric gets up. Starts to feed the fire.

You've always got to keep it alight. Ralph said.

Eric I know.

Sam I bet it comes out of the dark. I bet the beast comes out of the dark.

Eric How do you know?

Sam I bet it does.

Eric There isn't any beast. (*But he isn't at all sure about this.*) Don't be stupid.

Sam Don't nod off, will you? Or it'll come. It'll creep up behind you and . . .

Eric Shut up, will you?

Sam turns over.

There isn't any beast.

Sam Great big hairy thing. With claws. And talons. Like a – (*He stops.*) Oh God.

Eric What?

Sam I'm scared now.

Eric You see.

Sam There isn't really. (*But he sounds doubtful.*) Really there isn't.

Eric Are you sure?

Sam Sure.

Pause.

Eric Are you asleep?

Sam No.

44

Eric You're not scared are you?

Sam Of course I'm not. I'm going to sleep.

Eric Why aren't you asleep?

Sam Because you keep asking me stupid questions!

  Pause.

Eric Are you asleep now?

  *There is no answer. Sam is breathing steadily. Eric
  settles down.*

  Down at the front Ralph stirs.

Ralph Where are they?

Piggy Pig of course.

  Pause.

They're after pig.

Ralph They're always after pig. But do they catch any I'd
like to know.

Piggy They see 'em all right . . .

Ralph They stalk them and all that. They creep up behind
them in the trees. But do they catch them? That's what I'd
like to know. Hunters. Look at that shelter. I ask you.
Look at it.

Piggy You got to have a plan for shelters. Drawings.

Ralph You've got to have some help, I'll tell you that.
Shelters are difficult.

Piggy We should a' made a drawing.

Ralph (*mimics*) 'We should a' made a drorin'!' With what
may I ask?

Piggy You're chief. You should have made them. At the meetings you should a' done.

Ralph They don't do anything at the meetings though, do they? They sit around and someone says 'Let's build a TV set!' and then they get bored and wander off. What do you want me to do about it?

  But he feels Piggy's silent reproach.

You can't always make people, you know. Let's get some sleep shall we?

Simon It's funny. We built them but we sleep out here. You can see the moon from out here. However bad it gets, you can always see the moon.

Ralph Yeah. Well . . .

Simon Do we need houses anyway? If it's hot do we need them?

Ralph We'll need something if it rains. And we need to be a bit civilized. We need to keep smart and decent. Look at you.

Simon Look at you.

Ralph I can't see me. I haven't got a mirror. But you look a fright.

Simon I look like you then.

Ralph How do you know?

  Pause.

Piggy I wish they'd come back. They shouldn't go off like that. Not at night. And at the meetings they're so stupid . . .

Simon Merridew's really bossy.

Ralph Can we get some sleep please?

Simon Why?

Ralph Because . . . we'll be tired in the morning.

Piggy Thass what my auntie says. 'Get some sleep or you'll be tired in the morning.' And you're not always.

Ralph You have to go to sleep at a certain time and get up at a certain time. Otherwise . . .

Simon Otherwise what?

Ralph I don't know. You have to. That's all.

Simon I'm never tired on this island. Never. It's funny.

Piggy It's you that's funny.

Simon I'm not.

Pause.

It's such amazing colours. And at night those huge fireflies. And the moon. Like a lamp. This sky's not like the sky at home.

Piggy The moon's just the moon as far as I'm concerned. And sky's sky. Wherever you are.

Simon I bet we came out of the sky. Years ago. I bet we came from the sky and invaded this planet. I bet we did.

But the others are asleep.

I get scared looking at the sky. I see things in it.

And then he too sleeps. Silence over the whole darkened stage. Then, from above, high up from the left, we see something drifting down. The dead parachutist. His fall should be preceded by no sound, only a distant flare, like a shooting star. And when he falls it should be a slow drift out of the darkness, like a spore carried on

47

*the wind. In fact, what is hanging on the parachute
hardly looks like a man at all, so horribly disfigured is
it. His face battered and bloody. His hands caught up in
the trails of the chute. At the very top of the ridge is a
twisted tree, massive in scale. It is in the branches of this
that the parachutist comes to rest. The chute trails off to
his left and his head hangs forward horribly. A silence.
Then Eric stirs. He turns upstage and sees the shadowy
figure, scarcely recognizable as human at all, its face
almost blown away by the crash. Eric's so scared he can
hardly move. Then, terrified lest the vision start to life,
he leans across to Sam.*

Eric Sam –

Sam Uh?

Eric Sam . . . oh . . . Sam . . .

Sam Uh?

Eric It's here.

Sam What?

Eric Sam . . . the beast . . . Sam . . .

Sam Don't be stupid . . .

Eric I'm not. I wish I was. Oh Sam. Please. Look –

Sam Look – (*and he turns. Sees the figure in the tree. As
terrified as his brother.*) Oh my God!

Eric It is.

Sam It is what?

Eric The beast.

Sam Eric –

Eric It is, isn't it? Isn't it? Look.

Sam I daren't look.

Pause.

Has it seen us?

Eric I don't know.

Sam We must talk quietly.

Eric Aren't we talking quietly now?

Sam It mustn't hear us.

Eric I can hardly hear you, Sam.

Sam And warn the others . . .

Eric I'll shout . . .

Sam Don't shout.

Pause. They are both paralysed with fright.

It'll hear us.

The parachute flaps in the wind. Beyond the gauze the figure is horribly vague.

We'll have to crawl down the hill. And warn the others.

Eric Through all those trees?

Sam We'll have to.

Eric In the dark?

Sam What else can we do?

Eric What about the fire?

Sam One of us better stay here.

Eric I'm not staying here. Not with that.

Pause.

Sam We'll both go then. The fire'll keep it away.

Eric I'm scared.

Sam Don't be stupid. There's nothing to be scared of.

Eric I thought you said there was.

Sam Well there is. But you may as well be brave about it. Even though you are scared. Come on.

Eric I'll put some wood on the fire.

Sam Don't. Don't do anything.

Pause.

Come on!

And on their bellies, they start to crawl to their left, and down the incline of the stage, Eric a little way behind Sam. After a while Sam stops.

Eric Where are we?

Sam I don't know. I don't know everything.

Eric You do.

Sam I'm only your brother when it comes down to it.

Pause.

Eric Is it following us?

Sam I can't hear it.

Eric I think I heard it.

Sam Eric –

Eric Listen!

And far over on the left hand side of the stage we see Jack and Roger. Like all the others, some of their uniforms survive, but the length of their hair, the filth on

*their faces and perhaps more than all this, their manner,
suggests they are natives, not guests, of the island. They
are carrying wooden spears.*

Jack (*whispers to Roger*) Keep back!

Roger Did you hear it?

Jack What?

Roger The pig. It's in the bushes.

Jack There's something there.

They wait, all attention.

It's funny.

Roger What?

Jack When you're hunting . . .

Roger What?

Jack You know something's there. Hiding from you.

Roger Yeah. And you . . . (*He makes a stabbing
movement with his spear.*)

Jack Sssh! Listen!

*On the other side of the stage, Eric has got stuck. We
see him thresh against the bare stage.*

Follow me! And the others!

*And, behind the two leaders, in equally bizarre and
tattered clothes, come Maurice, Bill and Henry, all with
spears.*

Roger And if we find him . . .

Jack stabs downward with his spear.

Eric and Sam have frozen, hearing the noise of the hunters.

Eric I thought I heard voices.

Sam Don't be stupid. They're all on the beach.

Eric Maybe –

Sam What?

Eric Maybe the beast!

Sam Shut up! (*He's heard something.*) Sssh!

Jack It's that way! I heard it! It's that way! Come on!

And he runs off right, upstage of Eric and Sam. The others follow. Eric turns after Jack, aware of the noise but not able to see through the dark and the trees.

Eric It was! It was! It was!

Sam Shut up!

Eric Can't you hear it?

The line of hunters comes in from stage right, this time below Eric and Sam. Their spears are up in the dim light, and, led by Jack, they are screaming with excitement. They head for stage left.

Jack (*screams*) It's this way! Come on! It's this way!

Sam It's not the beast –

Eric It's the beast!

Sam It's the hunters!

Eric It's the beast!

Sam It's the hunters! It's –

The line of boys comes back from stage left.

Jack (*screams*) Kill it! I can seen it! Just there! Spread out and trap it! Hold it there! Hold it there!

*And the hunters, fanned out raggedly across the stage,
have sighted the pig. In ritual, slow, almost dance-like
steps they have started to move right. Eric, in blind
terror, his hands out in front of him, feeling his way
forward, weaves his way through these threatening
figures towards the beach.*

Sam (*screams*) Eric! It's only people! Eric!

Jack (*screams*) When I say 'charge' . . . wait for it!

Roger (*screams*) Wait for it!

Sam (*screams*) Eric!

Eric (*screams*) It's the beast!

Jack (*screams*) Cha-arge!

*And the hunters break into a run off to the right, as
Eric, totally panicked, heads for the front of the stage.
But as he does, Jack's hunters do a smart turn and head
back for the escaped pig, across the path of the terrified
Eric.*

(*screams*) It's that way!

Eric (*screams*) It's the beast!

*The hunters have now reached far stage left and, on a
command from Jack, stop as they did before, watching
for the pig, gone to ground in the darkness.*

Jack (*shouts*) Wait for it!

*Eric is now down front, shaking Ralph awake. Sam
follows Eric down.*

Eric (*screams*) Wake up! It's the beast!

Ralph What?

Eric (*shouts*) It's the beast!

Piggy Woch you on about?

Sam (*shouts*) Eric!

Eric (*screams*) It's the beast! It's up on the hill! I saw it! I saw the beast!

Piggy You saw it?

Eric (*screams*) It's there!

Jack (*screams*) Cha-arge!

Jack and the hunters storm off stage after the pig.

Ralph (*shouts*) Sam!

Piggy Did you see it?

Sam What?

Ralph You know what?

Sam Yes.

Offstage Jack screams wildly.

Jack Throw! Kill it! Kill it! Spill its blood!

Sam I saw it. I saw the beast. We both did. What was that?

Piggy Sounded like an animal.

Ralph Maybe it is an animal.

Piggy What is?

Ralph The beast.

Eric It was sort of . . . sitting . . .

Ralph has got up and is looking back into the darkness.

Ralph It could be a tiger or something.

Sam You can't see it. The moon's gone in.

Simon We should try and see what it is.

Ralph What?

Simon See what the beast is. Look at it. And then . . . then maybe someone would come, you see.

Ralph Would they? I don't know.

Piggy We should call a meetin'.

Sam Blow the conch.

Ralph Shall I then?

Piggy Where are they though? You see –

Ralph What?

Piggy Suppose we blew it and they didn't come. What then?

Jack and the hunters re-enter far stage left with the dead pig.

Jack Did you see?

Roger We saw.

Jack Did you see how I got him?

All We saw.

Jack It was my spear went in. I went . . . wham . . . and . . .

Maurice Right up his ass!

He mimes the pig's discomfort. They laugh.

Bill Oh, we saw.

Jack The sides of our spears are sharp. Use the sides of your spears.

Maurice There's a man. On my uncle's farm. He kills the chickens. He just goes – (*twirls with his right hand*) with his right hand. On their necks. Just like that.

They laugh.

They're dead all right. Super dead.

Jack Smell it!

Bill What? What?

Jack Pig. Can't you just smell it. (*He digs his hand in the blood of the animal and holds it up.*) This is the soul of the pig.

Henry Yea-aah! Yea-aah!

Jack Who's going to be first?

Bill First to what?

Jack To be blooded. No, better than blooded. This is better than blooded. Who's going to be first to be baptized?

Roger Baptized nothing . . .

Jack What?

Roger This is . . . (*mimes idiot gibbering*) Devil worship, my man.

Jack Yes? Roger? You want?

Maurice Massa he want!

Roger I crave it master!

Maurice Go on then!

Jack On your face . . .

Roger On my face, master!

Jack Can you take it?

Roger I can take it.

Jack You can take it?

Roger I can take it, master!

And Jack smears blood on Roger's face.

Maurice (*shouts*) Yea-aah!

Henry (*shouts*) Yea-aah!

All (*shouting*) Yea-aah!

Jack And now you – and then you – and then you! And then we'll take the pig back to the camp. Won't we? Eh? Can't you just see their faces?

All (*shouting*) Yea-aah!

Down on the beach at the front the little group have drifted apart, nervous at the continued absence of Jack and the others.

Ralph What are they doing though?

Piggy Go on, Ralph. You blow it.

He passes the conch to Ralph.

Ralph Why don't you?

Piggy I can't. Look, I'm scared of him. That's all. I'm scared.

Ralph That's no reason not to have a meeting though, is it?

Piggy I don't know.

Ralph What's to be scared of?

Piggy He hates you.

Ralph Who? Jack?

57

Piggy Yeh. 'e 'ates you.

Ralph Why should he hate me? Listen. He's got his hunters. Hasn't he?

Eric Suppose the beast hears it?

Sam Maybe it'll come . . .

Eric Sam –

Sam It'll come to the meeting!

Eric 'Hullo beast! Do you want to say something?'

Sam 'Yeah. I'd like to eat you.'

Ralph Look –

Sam Blow it! Blow it if you want!

Ralph I'll blow.

Piggy Ralph –

But Ralph has blown, a long, sweet note.

There.

Pause.

Now you done it!

Up on the hill we see Jack signal to the others to stop their work.

Maurice What was that?

Jack Him and his stupid shell.

Maurice We ought to go . . .

Jack Why?

Maurice We just ought.

Jack We're busy aren't we? (*He is hacking off the*

58

creature's head.) He said we'd never. He said we'd never catch one. And we did. A good, big, fat one.

Roger He'll eat it won't he?

Maurice Yes, but –

Roger Of course he'll eat it. He likes meat. Everyone likes meat. It's better than bananas anyway. And that jelly stuff.

Jack Let him eat crab if he doesn't like it. We'll have pig. Pig makes you strong.

They are listening to him.

And you are strong if you kill pig. Everything you kill makes you strong. But you have to have killed it. Not just eat it. All of us – we killed it. So we're in a gang, aren't we?

Maurice But still . . .

Jack Still what?

Bill Meetings are meetings.

Jack We'll go to his meeting. When we're ready.

Down at the front, Ralph, Piggy, Simon, Sam and Eric are waiting for a response to the conch.

Simon They're hunting. They won't listen when they hunt.

Sam Why should hunting stop you listening?

Simon You listen to that funny noise in your head when you hunt. I listen to it sometimes. It's like the sea you hear through a shell. But not the real sea. Like it's blood or something. Pounding away in your head.

Jack There. I got it. See? That's my head. (*Holding his spear. He forces it down into the earth.*) And this is where I killed it. This marks the spot where I killed it. Whenever we kill a pig we'll do that. We'll put the head where we killed it. We'll plant it, sort of. If you get to be good hunters and can hunt, you can do that. And the head will be special. It'll grow almost because we've planted it and set it up on a spear like the head on the castle wall, you remember and it'll keep away the . . . (*he is forcing the pig's head down on to the upturned spear shaft*) beast. Eh? (*Stands back.*) That's for you, beast.

Roger (*screams*) Ye-eaah!

Jack (*screams*) Ye-eaah!

All (*screaming*) Ye-eaah!

Piggy You've woken 'im now!

The lit'lun sits up very suddenly, awake with the speed of the young.

Look at 'im. 'e's awake!

Ralph What's he doing?

Piggy Gawd knows! (*Crossing to Perceval.*) Now you don't go toilet! Not 'ere. On the beach. You see? Thass where you go, innit?

Perceval stares at him.

Ainch yoo got ears?

Perceval I heard the shell.

Piggy You was dreaming.

Ralph Go back to sleep.

Perceval Can't sleep.

Ralph Well try.

Perceval Did I hear the shell, Ralph?

Ralph Maybe. I don't know. How do I know what you heard?

Pause.

I'll blow it and they'll come. I'll blow it once more.

At the back of the stage, in the half dark, the hunters have slung the headless carcass of the pig on to a pole.

Piggy Ralph –

But Ralph is preparing a vast intake of breath.

Ralph –

Ralph is raising the conch to his lips.

(*shouts*) Ralph!

But as Piggy cries out, Ralph blows. The noise swells and the hunters, who have been snaking down to the front in a long line, come out of the darkness, bursting into the light of the beach. They swing the pig's carcass down like a gage of battle before the others.

Hunters (*chanting loudly*) Kill the pig! Spill its blood! Kill the pig! Spill its blood!

Piggy rounds on them.

Piggy (*shouts*) Shut up cancher!

Hunters Kill the pig! Spill its blood! Kill the pig!

Piggy (*shouts*) Iss a meetin'!

A silence.

Jack It's a what, fatso?

Piggy You got blood on you.

Jack Blood. Haven't you ever seen blood?

Piggy Iss a meetin'.

Jack At night?

Piggy Yeh. At night.

Ralph Sam 'n' Eric saw the beast.

Jack They what?

Ralph Saw the beast.

Jack indicates the bloody corpse on the floor. Pause.

It had eyes. It had great, big black eyes.

Jack There isn't necessarily a beast.

Ralph They saw it.

Jack You're just trying to spoil it. I killed the first pig. And now you're trying to spoil it. (*A flash of childishness after the moment of power and strangeness up on the hill.*) I bring home the bacon. And you say it's the beast.

Ralph Jack –

Jack We killed our first pig. Can't you see? We speared it. Up there. It was dark. And we hunted it through the trees and I could see its eyes!

Simon Imagine what it's like being chased. Imagine!

Jack No thanks.

Pause.

We killed it. That's all.

Ralph That's good. It is good.

Jack Well then?

Ralph But it's not –

Jack What?

62

Ralph Simon –

Simon has wandered almost to the edge of the beach area. He turns, still with that spaced-out look.

Simon If you go up the mountain. If you go up to it. And don't wait for it to come to you then . . .

Perceval Then what?

Simon Then you're ready for it. And you recognize it. You see? (*He starts off into the darkness of the trees.*)

Ralph (*shouts*) Simon!

Jack (*shouts*) No! No!

This keeps Ralph in the circle of the beach.

You don't call him. You listen to me. It's a meeting. Isn't it? And I've got the shell haven't I? If there is a beast, if there is a beast up there by the fire . . . (*pause*) let's hunt it.

Ralph Well –

Jack Or are you scared?

Ralph 'Course I'm not scared.

Jack Right. Come on then.

Ralph All right then.

Piggy Ralph –

Ralph Shut up can't you?

Jack He's scared he'll be left here.

Ralph We can –

Bill What?

Ralph Bring back fire.

Maurice Fire from de mountain!

Henry Carry it down, you mean?

Ralph Yeah. Bring back fire from the mountain. And we can build a fire down here. If the beast's there. We can build our own fire and keep it going day and night.

Bill We could though couldn't we?

This idea has got them excited.

Maurice And cook food on it.

Henry We could though couldn't we?

Ralph We could. Right here on the beach, with the shell and everything we could build a fire and cook –

Maurice (*shouts*) Yeeeaah!

Bill (*shouts*) Yeeaah!

All (*shouting*) Yeeaaahhh!

Jack And we'll dance!

This is said to trump Ralph's notion. People don't quite get it. Jack continues.

We'll dance!

(*with passion*) Just like when we killed the pig. We'll all dance. We'll dance. (*Going up to the carcass.*)

Piggy Woss all that in aid of?

Jack, the uncompromising leader, is cornered suddenly. His anger at being trapped turns on Piggy.

Jack A dance, fatso.

Piggy Like savages do.

Jack I don't know about savages. Like we do. Like

everyone here could do. Apart from you, fatso, because you couldn't dance. All you could do was shake your blubber!

Maurice Ah am de savage man! I do de dance of –

Jack (*shouts*) Shut up! (*Pause. Looking round the group*) You will dance. I bet you. I bet you will. If we ever corner the beast. And look into its eyes and stare right down into its guts like you do when you're hunting and staring out the pig. You'll dance. And it won't be funny I can tell you boys. You'll go – (*he steps. Very slow and menacing*) Ai ai ai ee ouuuu!

> *No one's laughing now. His manner has compelled them to silence.*

Ai ai ai eeouuu! (*looking round*) And what's funny about that?

Ralph Nothing. Look I'm sorry if I –

Jack Anyone can laugh at my dance. But it means they're scared I think. Scared of the beast.

Ralph I'm not scared of the beast. I told you I'm not.

Jack I think you are. I think you're scared of it.

Ralph Look I told you. We'll go to the beast and bring fire away from it and –

Jack And we'll dance. We'll dance my dance.

Ralph Why aren't you happy if you're not thinking of the things to do? Why does everything else seem like second best to you? I don't care. I honestly don't care. But fair is fair you know. I was voted. I was voted for. And that's democratic. Why isn't that enough for you? Why do you always have to be in charge?

Jack Because –

This has brought their hostility out into the open.

(*shouts*) Because I killed the pig OK?

Pause.

Do you want to go then? Or are you scared? Are you chicken?

Ralph I'm game.

Roger I'm game, old chap.

Ralph What's that supposed to mean?

Roger Nothing, old chap.

Piggy You mustn't go.

Jack You've got a lit'lun to look after. You'll be all right.

Jack, Ralph and Roger head off in search of the beast.

Bill Where did Cambourne go?

Henry Don't know.

Maurice To the loo.

Laughter.

Meanwhile, Simon is centre stage, near the pig's head.

Simon My mind isn't right. It isn't. I'll have one of my goes if I'm not careful. My mind – (*He turns. Calls.*) Ra-alph!

Jack signals to his troupe to stop. They do so.

If Ralph was here . . . when I was eight I think . . . when I was eight I went down to the country and there . . . there was this horse in a field and . . . (*stops. Calls*) Ra-alph!

Pause. The three in search of the beast have moved on again but Jack signals with a brief ululation for them to stop.

68

If Ralph was here – Ralph would know. (*He stops. The faint moonlight catches the pig's head. It's right behind him and he hasn't seen it in the darkness. Freezes with fear. A whimper*) Oh. Oh no.

Jack signals his troupe on again and just as he does so, Simon calls.

(*shouts*) Ra-alph!

Jack calls to them to stop. They do so.

Simon is in front of the pig's head.

It's blood. And it's flies. It's blood. (*He starts to reach for the head.*) That head. That head. When I was eight I saw a man kill a bird. And I thought . . . Merridew says I don't pull my weight. Funny. Why should you pull weight? Eh, Piggy? Piggy? (*He is touching it with a thrill of horror.*) Those are flies. There's blood and there are flies. It's not my fault there's blood and flies is it? You look stupid come to that. (*He starts to work the pig's mouth, like a puppet's.*) 'Oh no I don't!' 'Oh yes you do!' 'You're a bad boy do you hear me!' (*Starting to giggle.*) Like Jenkins on that picnic. 'You're no go, boy!' 'You're no go!' 'I'm not no go, sir!' 'Oh yes you are – you're an ignorant, silly, little boy! And I know you are because I'm the beast! You hear me! I'm the beast!' (*He has scared himself. Starting to feel the fit coming on him.*) You're not. You're not. Pig's head on a stick. You're just a silly . . . (*very scared*) I feel funny. I'm going to . . . don't make me have a turn, sir, will you? Please don't let me have a turn, sir. Ralph! Ralph! (*And the fit starts. He begins reaching out for the head then falls, feet drumming on the earth, choking.*)

Ralph is near enough, in the darkness, to hear something, even if it isn't the whole story.

Ralph (*calls*) Hullo!

No answer.

Simon?

Still no response.

Jack (*calls*) Ralph?

Ralph I thought I heard a noise.

Jack What kind of a noise?

Ralph A sort of choking.

Jack In the trees?

Ralph They're so thick. You can't see a yard in front of your face.

Jack Want to go back?

Ralph No. (*Pause, then gently, trying to make peace between them.*) Jack –

Jack What?

Ralph Jack – why –

Jack Why what?

Ralph Nothing.

Jack What though?

Ralph We've got to have a fire. And shelters. We've got to be rescued. We've got to let people know we're here. Haven't we? That's all I'm trying to say. I'm not trying to . . .

Jack You are scared.

Ralph I'm not.

Jack You sound scared.

Ralph I'm not.

But in truth the dark and the trees are frightening them all.

Roger Are you there?

Ralph I heard a noise that's all. Let's stay very still. Very, very still. For just a bit, OK?

Jack You're just scared of going on.

Ralph I'm not. I'm not.

> *They stay stock still in the dark as, to Ralph's left, not far away, Simon lies prone in front of the pig's head.*
>
> *Down on the front stage, where the beach is, Piggy and the others are waiting.*

Piggy If we put a stick in the sand we could make a sundial.

Henry Not now we can't.

Piggy Why not?

Henry How can you have a sundial when there's no sun?

Piggy I mean when there is sun, stupid.

Henry Why do you want a sundial anyway?

Piggy To know the time a' course.

> *Pause.*

Iss useful to know the time. For meals and things. Woch you doin'?

> *Bill is playing with a pile of reddened earth, daubing it across his face.*

Bill It's earth. We put it on sometimes when we go hunting.

Piggy Real big hunters eh?

Bill Well? So what?

Piggy You can't be unless . . .

Bill Unless what? Why can't we be?

Maurice It goes with de blood! (*He smears some on Piggy's face.*)

Piggy That's just stupid.

Bill Why is it stupid? It's better for hunting.

Piggy It's –

Maurice De Piggy don't like it!

Henry Because he is a friend of the pig! (*Kicking the carcass.*) This your friend then?

Piggy They bin gone a long time . . .

Back up on the hill the three figures are still waiting.

Jack I'm going to give the signal to move in a minute.

Ralph Go on then! I don't mind.

Jack Just for a minute there, I thought you'd had enough.

Ralph Well you don't need to worry about that.

And Jack gives the signal. They move off. They are out of Simon's reach now, nearing the upper part of the stage.

I can see something.

Jack Where?

Ralph Ahead.

Jack It's hot isn't it?

Ralph Feels sticky. Like it was going to rain.

Roger What's happening?

Ralph I can see something.

Roger Yeah?

Ralph I'm not scared.

Jack Me neither.

Roger has dropped behind.

Coming then?

Ralph Of course.

They move up to where the fire is. Ralph grabs a burning brand from the fire. They stop, aware of the shape beyond the perimeter of the stage. But neither speaking.

Meanwhile, down at the front.

Maurice Can you sleep?

Piggy No.

Maurice I can't sleep.

Piggy My auntie says you don't if you're worried.

Maurice I just can't sleep.

Piggy They're taking so long.

And up at the top of the stage Jack, Ralph and Roger have seen the figure. It is swaying in the wind. And, just as the moonlight caught the pig's head, as Ralph stands there with the brand in his hand, the figure seems to move.

Ralph (*shouts*) It moved!

Jack (*shouts*) Ralph!

Ralph (*shouts*) It moved! It moved! Look at it! It's alive!

And at that moment the thunder breaks. A flash of lightning seems to bring the figure eerily to life. The three turn and run headlong down the mountain. They scream as they go and their screams are echoed by the thunder and lightning as the storm breaks.

(*screams*) It moved! It's alive! It moved!

They are at the bottom of the hill among the boys waiting on the beach.

(*screams*) There's a beast and it's alive and it moved!

Jack (*shouts*) It moved! It's alive! It is!

Roger (*shouts*) It's alive!

Piggy (*shouts*) Don't all speak at once!

Jack (*shouts*) It moved!

Pause.

Ralph It did.

Jack He ran away.

Ralph What did you do then?

Jack Only when you did.

Perceval Did it have teeth?

Ralph It did move.

The thunder breaks again.

Perceval I'm frightened. It's thunder . . .

Ralph You mustn't be frightened . . . (*But he is finding it hard to be convincing.*) It's only . . .

Jack What?

Ralph And look! (*He holds out the burning brand from the fire.*) We have fire. Down here.

Jack Just fire won't do it.

Ralph Get wood!

Jack Just fire's not enough.

Ralph Go on then. Get wood.

Maurice For what? For cooking or for smoke?

Ralph For everything. Does it matter?

Jack Of course it matters. For cooking. We'll cook pig.

Bill We're getting it.

Henry There's wood here. By the shelters.

Ralph But quickly. Before the rain comes!

Jack They can hear you!

> *Ralph ignores this. The group is suddenly animated.*
> *They get brushwood and sticks from the dark edges of*
> *the stage. Ralph puts the brand from the fire to it.*

Piggy Careful! Not too much!

Henry What did you carry, Piggy?

Piggy We don't want it like last time do we?

Maurice There's some here too . . .

Ralph Pile it up carefully!

Jack They can hear you!

Roger It's catching!

Bill And it's OK.

Sam Because the sand –

Eric Means it doesn't –

Sam Spread –

Jack More wood then!

Piggy Steady on then!

Ralph Yes . . . we don't want to . . .

Jack (*shouts*) Hey! Look! (*He's dragging more wood on, quite a large fragment.*)

And the fire is catching. Quite dramatic.

Ralph Be careful!

Roger 'Be careful!'

Henry There's more here and it's . . .

Sam Dry. Come on it's –

Eric Dry. Twigs and –

Bill Green leaves too . . .

Ralph (*shouts*) Listen we better think what kind of fire! Don't you think?

Henry It's a fire isn't it?

Roger Does it matter what kind of a fire?

Piggy 'Course it matters, stupid. It matters what a fire's for doesn't it?

Maurice Dis fire for de pig!

Jack Yes. For the pig!

Ralph Listen . . .

Jack More wood! Come on! More wood!

Bill Here's a whole branch!

Sam And there's a –

Eric Trunk here!

Perceval Can I put something on?

Ralph You've got to listen!

Jack To what?

Piggy You got to listen to him. And to what the fire's for!

Bill Put this round the edge, build it up round the edge then we can sling the pig across!

Roger Roast it! Across the fire! Roast it!

They have built up a wall round the edge of the fire, with rocks from the beach. All absorbed in the game.

Piggy This isn't right! Puttin' the whole pig on the fire?

Roger Shall we put just your leg then?

Bill Just his leg!

Roger He'd crisp up nicely!

Piggy Get off.

Maurice (*shouts*) Let's eat de pig! Hey!

And as they start to pull the carcass towards the flames Jack starts a handclap. The others join in with this.

Jack (*shouts*) Cut it! Slice at it! Burn it quicker! Who's hungry?

All (*shouting*) We are!

This does not include Ralph or Piggy. Though Piggy goes towards the meat as the group surround the animal, hacking pieces of it off with their spears and

77

throwing it on the flames, leaping up in the darkness.

Jack (*shouts*) Who's hungry?

All We are!

Ralph And what'll you do afterwards, eh? After you've all had a fire and cooked . . . that thing . . . and . . .

Jack Afterwards? What'll we do afterwards?

Ralph and Jack are now a little away from the fire as the group hack at the pig behind them.

Afterwards we'll dance!

Ralph This is a meeting!

Jack These 'meetings' of yours. They're quite good aren't they? When you want your own way – you get up and you shout 'It's a meeting!' Well what is a 'meeting' I'd like to know!

Ralph This! This is a meeting.

Jack Oh is it though? Is it? I thought it was a feast! If it's a meeting where's that shell of yours?

Ralph It's . . . (*He realizes he hasn't got it. Somewhere between the appearance of Sam and Eric and the trip to the mountain, it appears to have been lost.*)

Piggy Iss 'ere . . . iss 'ere somewhere . . . It can't a' got lost! We kept it in a special place din't we? For meetin's! Iss 'ere somewhere . . .

Jack Look at him! Look at him!

Ralph Jack –

Piggy is rooting around in the darkness on his knees. The others are absorbed in the fire.

Jack It's here! You don't even keep track of it anymore.

It's here. I've got it! (*From the tatters of his uniform, he draws the conch, having put it there on the way up to the mountain.*)

Ralph That may be. But a meeting's a meeting and I'm chief.

Jack Chief of what, eh?

Ralph So give me the shell.

Jack Why should I?

Ralph Because a meeting's a meeting. Look don't you want shelters and don't you want –

Jack What have shelters got to do with it?

Ralph Give me the conch!

Jack Go on then. You take your stupid conch!

And he throws it, petulantly, at Ralph. Ralph goes to catch it but misses and it falls into the fire.

Piggy (*shouts*) You stupid, stupid, stupid little boy!

He and Ralph head for the down stage side of the fire and scrabble for the conch with sticks, dragging it from the flames.

Jack Your stupid shelters come to that –

Ralph Don't say 'my stupid shelters' . . . don't . . .

Jack Your stupid, stupid . . .

Ralph (*shouts*) Well what do you want to do? Eh? What do you want to do?

Jack Me? (*A sudden, powerful savagery about him.*) I want to dance. I want to eat and dance.

Roger I vote we feast and dance.

Maurice I vote wid de feet! Ah am votin' wid my big feet! Like Jack done!

Ralph But you must (*shouts*) vote!

Piggy Hands up who wants –

Maurice Ma hands are up! Dey are in de air!

Henry Hands up!

Ralph (*shouts*) You've got to vote!

But the movement has started to follow Jack's lead.

Roger Can't you see? This is voting!

Maurice Ah am votin'! Dis de ballot box!

Jack It's pig time! Come on! (*chants, loudly*) Kill the pig! Spill his blood!

All (*chanting loudly*) Kill the pig! Spill his blood!

And the circle closes in round Maurice, clowning in an exaggerated fashion. This dance moves all the way across the stage, with different boys taking the role of the pig, and each time the group closing in on the pig. The shouts become regular and ritualized.

During this we see Simon, up in the centre area in front of the pig's head, recover, and start to move up to the top of the stage and the dying fire. When he gets there, dazed, he picks up a smoking brand from the fire and looks towards the tree. As he does so, the parachutist's head swings left and we see the whole of the exposed face, ghastly, covered in blood. Simon turns to look down towards the beach and screams.

Simon (*screams*) It's a man! That's all! It's a man that got killed! It's a body! That's all it is! There isn't a beast! There's a man! A man that got killed!

*But the dancers below don't hear him. He's left, like
some Cassandra, screaming his message to nothing.
They are wildly absorbed in the dance.*

Jack (*chants loudly*) Kill the pig! Cut his throat! Spill his
blood!

All (*likewise*) Kill the pig! Cut his throat! Spill his blood!

*The thunder breaks again. The storm builds and builds
as the scene progresses.*

Ralph (*screams*) It's rain! Can't you hear the thunder?
What about the shelters?

Jack (*shouts*) You shout now! Come on! You shout! and
join our dance!

Roger (*chants loudly*) Kill the pig! Spill his blood!

All (*likewise*) Kill the pig! Spill his blood!

Piggy (*shouts*) Go on then! Go on, Ralph!

Ralph (*chants*) Kill the pig!

All (*likewise*) Spill his blood!

Ralph (*again*) Kill the pig!

All (*likewise*) Spill his blood!

Jack (*screams*) Ayyyyyy!

*Jack's glee at having Ralph on his terms is total. He
grabs earth and smears his face. A moment of terrifying
power. But as he does so, and as the circle closes in, this
time with no one at the centre, Simon starts to stagger
down from the mountain. Above the thunder we hear
him scream.*

Simon (*screams*) You must listen to me! There isn't a
beast! There's a man! and the man's dead! He looks
horrible but it's only a man! You mustn't think there's any

81

more than that! (*This brings him to the edge of the beach.*)

   Roger turns from the dancers.

Maurice (*shouts*) Kill the beast! Spill his blood!

   Simon, exhausted, falls, just at the edge of the beach.

Simon (*screams*) It's a man!

All Kill the beast! Spill his blood!

Simon (*screams*) It's a man!

All Kill the beast! Spill his blood!

   And now, they are moving in on the prostrate form of Simon, stabbing and kicking as they do so.

Simon (*screams*) It's a man! It's a man!

All Kill the beast! Spill his blood!

   They are pushing him now, kicking and shoving. Simon, badly wounded, staggers towards the fire. Behind, the wind of the approaching storm that has been blowing throughout this climactic sequence fills the parachute on the hill up, so that the bloody grotesque figure seems to lift of its own volition and hang there, arms out, crucified above the trees. Then, as Simon falls below the flames, screaming with fear, and staggers out down front, beaten near to death, the figure behind falls back into the darkness of the trees.

Roger It's the beast! Kill the beast! Spill his blood!

All (*screaming*) Ay ay ay ay!

Jack Kill the beast! Spill his blood!

All (*screaming*) Ay ay ay ay!

   Simon, dragging tatters of his school clothes flaming behind him, falls at the front of the stage and the pack fall on him. There is no call now. His killing is silent, close, and the more horrible for that. Then the mass of bodies breaks back and we see Simon centre front, not moving. A long silence.

Jack It's dead.

Silence.

See? It's dead. It came out of the dark and now it's dead.

Ralph I said –

Jack What did you say?

Ralph I said . . . we were going to have a . . . meeting . . .

Jack We're not going to have any more meetings. And Ralph's not going to be chief any more. Anyone who wants can come with me. Out in the woods there. We'll feast and hunt and have fires and do anything we want. Who's coming?

No one moves. They are backing away from the body.

Ralph isn't chief any more. Put your hands up if you want me for chief. (*He stamps.*) See? That's how we'll do it! And I'll be chief. For ever and ever, amen.

Pause.

Come on. Come on then!

Pause. Still nobody moves. Jack turns on Ralph.

I hate you. You and your stupid shell. Look! I've still got it! (*He pulls it out of his tatters.*) But I don't want it. And I don't want you. I'm going away for good. And anyone who wants can come with me. OK? If you want you can join me!

Still no one moves. Jack moves back into the darkness. Silence after he's gone.

Piggy That was . . .

Ralph (*shouts*) Shut up!

Perceval That was the beast wasn't it?

No answer.

Wasn't it?

Ralph Listen everybody! (*Picking up the shell Jack has thrown down.*) You all heard the thunder. What Jack is saying is stupid. And now . . . we've got a good place . . . here . . . on the beach . . . this is serious what I'm saying. We've got to have . . .

Piggy Rules.

Ralph Rules. Like Piggy said. And we'll be rescued and . . .

In the half dark Roger starts up a chant, almost to himself.

Roger (*quietly*) Ay ay ay ayyy! Ay ay ay ayyy!

Ralph Stop that can't you?

Roger Why?

Ralph (*screams*) I said stop that!

Pause.

Jack's just . . . Jack's been just . . . he'll come back of course and . . .

Roger Kill the pig. Ay ay ay!

And, just offstage, in the darkness, we hear Jack answer the call, just as softly: 'Ay ay ay ayy!'

Ralph Now we're all going to stay and . . .

But Roger is melting into the shadows.

Roger!

Roger You look so pathetic with that shell. Like it's a hot water bottle or something.

And he's gone.

Ralph Come on the rest of you let's . . . Bill . . . (*Looking round. But he can't see him.*) Where's Bill gone?

Sam He went –

Eric Somewhere –

Sam Don't know –

Ralph Where's Henry? Henry?

Piggy 'e was over there by the . . . (*Making a bold front.*) Come on then! It's a meetin' now! Come on! Where've you all got to?

And from the shadows: 'Ay ay ay!'

Maurice I was on the outside.

Ralph I was too.

Piggy I was. I din't . . .

Ralph Didn't what?

Piggy I didn't see anything.

Ralph Me neither.

Maurice Me neither. We was all shouting and then . . .

Ralph You're not going with them, are you?

Maurice No.

Pause.

Ralph We'll keep here. Us lot. We'll stay decent and we'll keep here. We'll keep the fire going. Look. Look over there. Look out to sea. Over there. There's a light. Isn't there? I'm sure there's a light.

Piggy Where?

Ralph There. Over there. I was sure I saw a light. There. Like a rocket or something. Look. Look over there. Into the sea. That way.

All that are left – Piggy, Sam and Eric, Perceval, Ralph – are watching. Unseen by them, Maurice is fading into the darkness. They strain their eyes in the dark.

Sam Where's Maurice gone?

Piggy Dunno.

Ralph Gone with the others.

Piggy Must a' done.

Ralph I was sure I did. I was sure I saw a light.

Pause.

Piggy That was Simon.

Ralph Shut up can't you?

Piggy That was murder.

Ralph We . . .

Sam Weren't –

Eric There –

Piggy I was on the outside!

Ralph I was on the –

Piggy We was all on the outside. Weren't we?

Ralph I can't look at him.

Piggy Don't look at him then.

86

Pause.

There wasn't no light. Not really was there? Don't look at 'im then, Ralph. Look back the other way. Look at the island. We ought ter get some sleep.

Blackout.

Act Three

Brilliant light. Down at the front of the stage are Ralph, Piggy, Sam and Eric. Their shelter has deteriorated. There is a small fire. Time has moved on because the pig's head on the stick is now a skull and the last vestiges of the boys' clothes that we saw in Act Two have gone. They are all almost naked, and, even though Ralph and the others haven't decorated their faces, they have long hair and are much browner than they were. Up at the back, in the trees beyond the gauze, although this is not clearly visible, the parachutist, too, has rotted to a skeleton. All that can be seen of him is a bundle in the harsh twigs of the trees behind the cyclorama, like a huge rook's nest against the light of the sky behind.

Piggy Where are they?

Ralph They were along the beach. And then . . .

Piggy Then what?

Ralph I see them up there sometimes. Up by where the fire was.

   They both shiver. Ralph laughs bitterly. Hey, I could always blow on the conch. Pull them down in a flash!

Piggy Ralph –

Sam Let's go back to the shelters and –

Eric Sleep I don't –

Sam Like it out here. It's too –

Eric Hot.

Ralph We'll go in then if you like. Go in and sleep. (*Pause. He is listless. All his natural confidence in the society he has left behind has gone.*) Doesn't seem right to go to sleep in the day.

From the door of the rickety shelter, Perceval emerges.

Perceval My tummy feels funny. Where is everyone?

No one answers.

Why don't we go swimming anymore?

No one answers. Perceval goes back in.

We see Roger come out along the line of the hilltop, now harsh against the blue of the cyclorama. This is not the same Roger at all. All the wreckage of his schoolclothes gone, his face painted. He has a horrible sort of dignity about him as he stands looking down at the island.

Piggy What are they doin'? What are they plannin'?

Ralph I don't know.

Piggy I tell you one thing, Ralph. They don't get fire. We got fire. (*Cunning.*) The night a' the storm when it did rain you bet it rained up there.

Ralph Yeah.

Piggy An' we stayed out here din't we? You an' me. We kept the fire goin'. Din't we?

Ralph Yeh, in the end.

Pause.

Piggy An' their fire wen' out din' it? Mus' a' done.

Ralph I expect.

Piggy So what they bin livin' on these weeks? Raw pig?

Ralph I suppose.

Piggy Can't see 'em likin' that!

Ralph No.

Piggy What does 'e do with 'em up there?

Ralph I don't know. (*He looks up on the hill.*)

We see Roger patrol across the skyline. There should be nothing of the play acting about this. It's frighteningly adult.

They all paint their faces. And tie their hair back.

Piggy I could tie my hair back I s'pose . . .

Sam Like a girl!

Eric Like a –

Piggy What's wrong with –

Ralph Oh don't you start –

Piggy Sorry.

Ralph stops.

Ralph Wear your hair like that if you think you want to.

This moment of intimacy with Ralph softens Piggy.

There isn't a beast. Simon said it, the night he . . .

This silences them.

There isn't a beast.

Eric Isn't there?

And the mention of the night of Simon's killing has, curiously, made the reality of the beast possible.

I don't know. I wouldn't like to be up there anyhow. They

all must be . . . like it don't you think? If they're so close to it. They must be a bit like it. They –

We see Jack come out. He is dressed slightly differently to the others. He stands in the centre.

Eric There he is he's –

Sam Wearing a spear, he's –

Ralph Why are you so bothered about Jack? If he wants to hunt let him. If he wants to hunt and be stupid let him. Why should we bother about him? We don't need him.

Sam I'm going in the shelter . . . it's –

Eric Too hot here . . .

They start to drift, slightly listlessly, towards the shelters.

Ralph It's funny.

Piggy What is?

Ralph When we came . . .

Piggy What?

Ralph You felt you could go on. That the whole island was yours. And it's like it's shrunk. To this patch of beach and sands. Where we want to be smaller and smaller. To be safe.

Eric I'm going in the hut.

Ralph He hasn't got fire.

Piggy No.

Pause.

Ralph What would your auntie say?

Piggy I dunno.

Pause.

It was funny. At first I could imagine what she would say. I knew. I could 'ear 'er voice. But now I couldn't imagine. Wot she'd say or wot she'd . . .

Ralph When I was a really little kid – we were coming home from the sea. Because my dad was in the Navy. And we stopped by the side of the road and there were these horses and I thought . . .

Piggy What?

Ralph It doesn't matter now does it?

Piggy I'm going in.

Ralph I'll put wood on the fire. (*Looks up at the skyline.*) I wonder what they're doing.

Jack Roger and Bill come with me. Maurice and Henry stay here.

Maurice Why can't I come?

Jack You just can't.

Maurice I want to come.

Jack I say if you can or if you can't.

Maurice I know but . . .

Jack I say. Don't I? (*He taps his spear on the ground.*)

Roger You hear the chief. What the chief says. Eh, Chief? (*Something almost insolent in his manner.*) Are we going then, Chief?

Jack When I say.

Roger Of course. When you say.

Bill What are we going to do?

Jack We'll know when we get there.

Bill Was it just a man? Was that all it was? (*He looks nervously up towards the indistinct shape in the trees behind them.*)

Jack It was a man. But. (*He has total authority.*) Sometimes the beast takes the shape of a man. And sometimes it's like an animal. A horrible animal. And sometimes it looks like a little boy. Like an ordinary little boy. Like the one who came into the circle that time. It can take all sorts of shapes. So you have to be careful. And it'll be back.

Maurice What are you going to do?

Jack We're going to teach them a lesson.   ·

Roger Shall we . . . (*He mimes a vicious movement with his spear*) Like that? Shall we? (*A smile.*) How they'd squeal.

Jack Leave the fat one to me.

Maurice What are you going to do?

Jack Chief.

Maurice What are you going to do, Chief?

Jack Chiefs don't have to say. Chiefs decide. (*He taps his spear on the ground.*) I've spoken. Come on then!

They move down stage. In almost ritual military order. A step. A pause. Then another step.

Ralph comes out of the shelter. From within we hear Piggy's timorous voice.

Piggy Are they there? I'm scared, Ralph!

Perceval What's happening?

Ralph You just all keep quiet now.

*But the words won't quite form. Perhaps they're doing
something worse, more frightening than stupid.*

On the hill, Jack calls.

Jack When I call you stop! OK?

They move one step further. Jack calls.

From inside the shelter we hear Percival call.

Perceval I was sure I heard something.

Ralph You didn't hear anything. Just the birds. (*He
shivers and goes in the shelter.*)

*Jack moves down past the pig's skull on the spear in the
centre of the stage.*

Jack This is where we first killed pig.

Roger His bones are white.

Jack The pig's bones are white! When you pass here . . .

Bill What?

Jack Spit!

Bill What?

Jack (*shouts*) Spit! Can you hear me? Spit for luck!

Roger You heard! You heard what the chief said! Spit!

Pause. Then Bill spits. Jack turns on Roger.

Jack And you!

Roger 'Course. (*He spits.*) You going to spit?

Jack I'm going to –

Roger You should . . .

Jack You first.

Roger I did.

Jack Again.

Roger 'Course! (*He gobs up. Quite a lot. Laughs as he does it. But the insult is hard to spot as he adds*) Lot of it! Eh, Chief? Lot of it?

Jack Yeah. (*He spits.*) That's for luck. (*He gives the call sign.*)

They move off.

Roger (*mimicking voice*) Hey! A lickle house!

Jack (*calls softly*) Piggee!

From within we hear Piggy's frightened voice.

Piggy Ralph! I think I heard something . . .

Jack Come on! Come on! Piggee!

Piggy Ralph! They're out there!

Ralph Don't be stupid! They're . . . (*But his voice dies away.*) Is that you? Is that you, Jack?

Roger Piggee!

Ralph If you want a fight we'll . . .

Jack Piggee! (*He laughs.*) Come out then! Come on out, blubber!

Ralph You come on if you're so brave! You come on in!

Jack What's so great about your shelter then? What's so great about this shelter when it comes to it? It can be knocked in. Easy.

Ralph Can it though? Eh? Can it?

Piggy Jus' 'cos we ain't ready with weapons. Jus' 'cos we're bein' sensible. You –

95

Jack (*screams*) Go for the pig! Go for the fat pig!

And all three set on Piggy. They grab his glasses.

Piggy (*screams*) Ralph! I can't see! Ralph! Help me!

The three break away from Piggy and, out in the open, Ralph tackles Bill. But Jack and Roger turn on him, and, using the handles of their spears, beat him off savagely.

Jack (*shouts*) Break up the camp!

With their spear handles they rake through the small fire, scattering it. Ralph comes up fighting again, but, without much support from the others, can do little. Jack triumphant.

(*screams*) Ay ay ay ayyyy! (*He gives his call.*) We will break your shelters whenever we want. And take your fire whenever we need. Because I'm the chief. And these are my hunters. You understand? (*Beating the ground with his spear. That dance step again.*)

Roger You hear him? You hear him?

They turn and go, giving the fire a last scatter as they leave.

Sam I got one –

Eric And I got one, I –

Piggy Ralph. They took my glasses. Why did they want to go and do that? I can't see a blind thing without my glasses.

Ralph momentarily distracted from the immediate fire problem. Angrily turns after them.

Ralph (*shouts*) Thanks for being so decent! (*Nursing his arm.*) They got me in the arm.

Piggy Ralph what we gonner do? I can't see a thing and . . .

Ralph The fire. Oh my God the fire. Come on you lot. Help!

Piggy I can't Ralph. I really can't see without 'em.

Ralph stares about him wildly, as up by the skull the raiding party stops and spits. Jack holds up the glasses. They turn on and head up towards the crest of the hill.

I can't help if I can't see . . .

Out of the debris of the shelter crawls Perceval.

Perceval What was that?

Sam It was them, stupid.

Perceval Was it Jack's lot?

Sam Much use you were.

Perceval Why did they do it?

Ralph We don't know. We don't know why they did it. But the fire's scattered, we have to . . .

Piggy That was why they wanted my glasses.

Ralph We have to get it going. (*He is kneeling by some smouldering timbers.*)

Perceval Why did they do that?

Ralph I don't know OK?

Perceval You're the chief.

Ralph Am I? I don't know about that either come to that.

The fire won't go. Ralph casts about for more twigs. But most of the firewood is used.

Chief of what? Chief of a few broken sticks. Chief of a few . . .

We see Jack and the others reach the crest of the hill. Jack turns and dances, triumphant, across the skyline.

There's the chief. Up there. You heard him. Him and his painted face.

Piggy He's not! He's not! You mustn't say that!

Ralph Why not? (*He gets up from the scattered fire.*) Look at it! Look at what I've got and . . . look at what he's done. (*Crossing to the shelter.*) It doesn't take long does it? It takes weeks or months to make something. To build it up from nothing. Slowly. And along they come with . . . and there it is, spread over the sand.

Piggy You mustn't say that, Ralph. The fire wasn't . . .

Ralph The fire was low, Piggy. We let the fire get low.

Piggy You mustn't say those things, Ralph. Ralph where are you?

Ralph Can't you see at all?

Piggy You're a blur. Thass all. A blur.

Ralph Can't you see me now? (*He moves closer and closer.*)

Piggy I toljer. Not without my specs.

Ralph's right up to him.

Ralph Now. Now can you see me?

Piggy You're too close now.

Ralph Now. Is that better? (*He's backing off.*)

Piggy Sort of . . .

Ralph Can you see my face?

Piggy Sort of. I can remember your face anyway. Your face ain't the point is it? The point is . . . the fire . . .

Ralph The fire's out.

Piggy Iss not dead.

Sam Don't go away fire!

Eric No don't go away fire!

Sam We need you fire!

Eric We need you!

Perceval I'm blowing!

Piggy Is it comin' up? Is it? I bet iss comin' up a bit innit? It always does a bit doesn't it?

Ralph It's no good, Piggy . . .

Perceval Piggy – what're we going to do?

Piggy Ralph'll think a'sunning. Woncher Ralph?

Ralph Will I? (*Suddenly angry, he turns to the figures on the hill.*) Thanks for taking our fire! Thanks so much! (*screaming*) Don't you want to be rescued? Is that it?

Perceval Won't we be rescued then?

Piggy How can we? Without smoke for a fire?

Perceval But you said we –

Sam Stop blubbing . . .

Perceval I'm not blubbing . . .

Eric You are.

Perceval I'm not.

Sam You are.

Perceval I'm not. I –

Ralph (*shouts*) Shut up can't you?

And now Perceval does start to cry in earnest.

Piggy Iss no good cryin'! That won't get the dog washed will it? Ralph's chief.

Perceval Is it war then?

Piggy I dunno. (*He's still kneeling.*) It's gone 'asn't it?

Ralph Yes.

Piggy Get the conch.

Ralph Why?

Piggy Why not?

Ralph What's the –

Piggy When we first come 'ere we blew it din't we? Din't we? That first day we blew it. When we had rules. Maybe if we blew it again . . .

Ralph What?

Perceval Would the rules come back if we blew it?

Piggy Blow it, Ralph. An' we'll have a meetin'. Just us.

Ralph Just us? (*But he crosses to the broken wreckage of the shelter, where the shell is kept. And he blows it. Long and loud.*)

Sam There are some in the woods still. Some lit'luns. They just stay there. They hide there.

Piggy It don't matter if it's just us, Ralph. A meetin' is a meetin'. So now we're havin' a meetin'. An' you say what we're going to do.

Ralph If we washed and changed. If we brushed ourselves up. If we didn't go like savages, with painted faces but in our proper uniforms. The ones we had when we came. The clothes we –

Sam I got a pair of socks we could –

Eric Wear socks and –

Sam Shoes. There are shoes somewhere.

Perceval We should wear hats.

Pause.

Piggy Socks an' what else eh? Sock's an' hats! Jus' go in our socks an' hats? You think that'll convince him, do yer? You think he goes for socks and hats?

Ralph I've got the conch!

Piggy I want to speak. This is just talk –

Perceval We could wear socks over our heads. Like caps.

Sam We should wear something that –

Eric Tells them we won't be –

Sam Messed around with –

Eric Carry a spear or something. There's a spear. A spear we used once when –

Piggy Gimme the conch! What use is a spear? Eh? I won't carry no spear. Did any of us ever carry spears? Was that what we did?

Ralph passes Piggy the conch. He has to grope for it.

I won't be able ter see anything I'll tell yer that. I'll be led like a dog to him won't I? But I'll go anyway. Even if you have to lead me like a dog. I'll go to him with this . . . (*holds up the conch*) and I'll tell the truth. Awful things bin

done on this island. Simon was killed. Simon was
murdered. I'll say that because that's the truth. An' I'll
say . . .

Pause.

I'll go to him with this conch in my hands. I'm going to
hold it out. 'Look –' I'm going to say – 'you're stronger
than I am and you haven't got asthma. You can see –' I'm
going to say – 'and with both eyes! But I don't ask for my
glasses back, not as a favour. I don't ask you to be a
sport,' I'll say, 'not because you're strong but because
what's right's right! Give me my glasses!' I'm going to say
– 'you got to!' (*Near to tears, he pushes the conch into
Ralph's hands.*)

Ralph Well. Let's then. Let's go to him.

Piggy I'll carry the shell.

Perceval Why?

Ralph Because –

Pause.

Because it's the conch and it's precious. It's the most
precious thing we've got. And he looks after it. That's his
job. OK?

Sam Look at this!

Ralph Leave it alone . . .

Sam Why? Didn't we wear these once?

Ralph Just leave it alone.

*Up on the rock, the stones are piling up. Jack, Maurice
and Bill are crouched over the fire with Piggy's glasses.*

Jack Is it alight yet?

Maurice It is, Chief.

Jack You see? I told you.

Maurice It's alright!

Jack And later . . . we'll feast. (*Beats the earth with his spear.*) And all the rest'll come to us. From out of the woods. You'll see.

Roger crosses to them.

Roger They look tiny down there. Shall we chuck stones at them?

Maurice You couldn't reach.

Jack Who says?

Maurice Ah am sayin' dis!

Jack That's a stupid voice. What's that voice supposed to mean?

Maurice Ah am de native Massa –

Jack Native? Native? What's that mean? Native?

Pause.

Maurice You heap big chief.

Jack I'm not 'heap big chief'. You call me chief with some respect and meaning. Not as a joke. Or are you making some kind of joke at my expense?

Maurice No. I'm –

Jack You've got to have respect for the chief.

Maurice I have. I –

Jack is very close to him.

Jack Have you though. Have you?

Maurice Don't, Merridew. I –

Jack 'Merridew.' 'Merridew.' Who's Merridew?

Pause.

I remember there was a boy called Merridew. But that was a long time ago. And on another island probably. I don't know about any boy called 'Merridew'. All I know is – I don't like your look.

Maurice I'm sorry. I really am. I –

Ralph We should go as we are. Not dress up. Even that way we're better than them. Come on. Everyone OK?

Perceval Can I hold on to someone too?

This is because Ralph is getting ready to lead Piggy.

Ralph Hold on to Piggy!

Sam We'll bring up the –

Eric Rear!

Sam We'll be right –

Eric Behind!

Perceval Can I hold on to you?

Ralph All form a line. If you like. Through the trees. All form a line.

Piggy I can't see a blind thing, Ralph!

Ralph Come on!

And he leads the weird troupe off. It twists this way and that, like a snake, right across the line of the stage. Watched from the hill by the hunters, shading their eyes against the harsh light.

Jack They've left the beach.

Roger They're into the trees. I've lost sight of them!

Maurice It's hot!

Bill The sun blinds your eyes.

Roger He'll be blind. Without his glasses.

Jack He'll have a job finding us.

Roger Keep a look out!

Henry Did you see? I think they were holding hands!

Maurice I see them!

Ralph Damn him with his spears and things. You hear me? Damn him and all of them. Look at it. What do they do with this?

Piggy I can't hardly see it, Ralph . . .

Ralph Do they fall down and worship it or something? Do they paint their faces and fall down in front of a pig's head?

Perceval I don't like it . . .

Ralph's group arrive at Jack's rock. They stop.

Ralph We want to speak to you.

Jack What about?

Ralph You stole Piggy's glasses.

Jack This is our end of the island. You don't belong here. You go back to where you were.

Ralph You stole Piggy's glasses and broke up our huts. And you had no right to do that. You had no right to come and steal our fire. We'd have given you fire. You hadn't the right to come and steal it.

Jack I told you. Go back to where you came from. (*He*

raises his hand. The chief.) This is our rock this is. This is Castle Rock this is. And we're safe up here. You stay down there.

Ralph It was a rotten thing to do.

Jack I don't know what you're talking about.

Ralph Why do you think you're so clever? I didn't come to make a war.

Jack Then what's the spear for?

Ralph To teach you a lesson if you try anything.

Sam and Eric step forward.

Jack Come on then! Teach me! Come on!

Jack steps down. The two circle each other, feinting. They shift their spears round so that they are toying with the blunt end of the weapon.

You see? You see what he's after?

Ralph I'm not after anything. I just came here because we want Piggy's glasses back. Without them we can't make fire. We can't –

Jack lunges. Ralph dodges. The tribe start to beat their spear handles on the ground.

Eric Don't touch him! Or we'll . . .

Jack You'll what?

Eric We'll teach you. We'll really teach you.

Ralph (*shouts*) Eric! Stay back!

Roger moves forward too.

Jack (*shouts*) Tie them up!

Sam You can't. You –

Roger (*shouts*) Tie them! You heard what the chief said!

Ralph (*shouts*) You bloody cheat and liar and thief!

All his hatred focussed on Jack. The two fight really furiously as the rest of the tribe, using strong creepers from the trees, tie up Sam and Eric.

Sam (*shouts*) You can't. You –

Eric (*shouts*) Can't it's not –

Sam (*shouts*) Fair you can't!

Roger Who said anything about . . . (*viciously tightening their bonds*) fair?

Piggy I did!

He has stepped out from the trees. His interruption makes a break in the struggle between Ralph and Jack. Everyone stops to look at the half-blind figure, coming alone into the space before the crest of the hill.

I did. And I got the shell to prove it.

Silence. They are all listening.

I got the conch. Ralph? Are you there, Ralph? You better listen anyway. And you, Jack Merridew, you better listen.

Pause.

Which is better – law and rescue or hunting and breaking things up? To have rules and agree or to hunt and kill like a pack of savages?

Ralph Piggy –

Piggy Woch you think you're doing eh? With them spears and stones? This says I got to be listened to. You hear me? This says we got something to hold on to so's we can remember who we . . . who we . . . are, OK? I remember an' remember all the good advice I got an' all. (*He walks up the hill.*)

Ralph Piggy –

Piggy Where are yer, Ralph? They'll listen. 'Course they'll listen. 'ere it is. An' I can't blow it like 'e can. But I can hold it up like this and see it shine and know iss something we can all agree on. And you may not like me but this is stronger than I am and more important!

Ralph This way –

Bill Over here!

Ralph The other way!

Roger No no no it's over here!

Piggy (*shouts*) Ralph!

Ralph (*shouts*) Leave him alone can't you?

Jack Standing up for your fat friend?

He lunges at Ralph. The fight starts again. Piggy, really almost blind, is panicked by the noise.

Piggy That you, Ralph?

Ralph (*shouts*) Over here!

Roger (*shouts*) No here!

And as Ralph is tied up with Jack, Roger steps forward and offers Piggy his hand. Piggy takes it.

Piggy That you, Ralph?

But Ralph is wrestling with Jack. Roger starts to lead Piggy towards the crown of the hill.

This your hand, Ralph?

Roger Yeah. Yeah. This is chunky Ralph you got hold of.

Pig.

As Piggy struggles in panic, Roger tightens his grip.

Piggy Let go! Let go cancher?

Roger What's the matter? I'm Ralph! I'm a good, good person. I believe in rescue. Wethcue and shlterth thatth me. And of course I believe in pwetty, pwetty, shellth!

Piggy Lissen –

Roger Come along pig. Pig pig piggy come along!

Bill Hey! Blind man!

Henry Blind man!

Maurice darts forward and buffets Piggy.

Maurice Blind man's buff!

Piggy (*screams*) Ralph!

But Jack and Ralph are locked on the ground.

Roger Blind man's buff!

Piggy (*screams*) Ralph!

Ralph (*shouts*) Piggy, this way!

Piggy (*screams*) I got the conch, Ralph! (*And as he staggers blindly about, buffeted from one to the other, getting nearer and nearer to the crest of the hill, he holds the shell up. Shouts*) Look at it you lot!

Roger (*shouts*) We can see it, fatso! We can see it! (*He twists it out of Piggy's grasp.*)

Now we see it! Now we don't!

The shell falls to the ground.

Piggy Where am I? I can't see. Where am I?

Roger On top of the mountain, blubber. Right on top of the mountain. (*He starts to push Piggy towards the edge.*)

Piggy Don't! Don't please! Don't push me! Don't –

Ralph (*screams*) Piggy!

Piggy (*shouts*) Ra-alph!

This last shout of his friend's name turns into a scream as Piggy falls off the high back of the stage. The scream is cut short by a heavy, curiously solid sound, as if a large weighted sack had hit the deck. There is a dead silence. Ralph starts forward . . .

Ralph Murderers! Murderers! Murderers!

Jack That's what you get, you hear me? That's what you get for coming here you hear?

He throws his spear. For real. It glances Ralph's side, hurting him quite badly.

Roger (*shouts*) See? See what you get?

Bill (*shouts*) Get out you hear?

And they are throwing stones. This should be serious stuff.

Ralph (*shouts*) Murderers! (*He dodges backwards, into the trees.*)

Jack (*shouts*) Wait!

They watch as Ralph crouches low, centre upstage.

He's gone in the trees. Wait.

Roger has come down. Jack and he stand, nervous of each other, scanning the line of trees.

What do you want?

Roger Look. I got the conch, Chiefy! I got the conch.

Jack The conch doesn't count at this end of the island. You know that.

Roger I know that. Hey! Catch! (*He tosses it at Jack.*)

Jack catches it.

Jack It doesn't count.

And, almost listlessly, as if he didn't want to touch anything Roger has touched, he tosses it back to Roger. The shell goes round the group again. But not as it did in Act One, in an optimistic spurt of physical activity, but from Roger out, and then back to Roger. Listless and awkward. Finally the last of the tribe tosses it back to Roger and he stands looking at it.

Roger Hullo again! (*to the others*) Shall I chuck it after him? (*He drops it.*) It's not very strong. Look! Look! (*He starts to chip at it with one of the stones.*)

The others gather round, impassively curious at this new development. Perhaps some vague tribal memory is stirring of how important the thing once was. As Roger gets to work it proves harder than he thought, and at the end he is hitting it really hard, almost in a frenzy. But once it's broken, it's not too hard to pound even more. By the time he has finished with the shell, it is powder.

The wind'll just blow it away. (*He throws it up in the air, almost, but not quite, deliberately aiming it at Jack. He crosses to Jack.*) Oh look, Chiefy! Some got in your eye!

Jack Get off –

Roger The chief's got to see straight! (*Attempts to wipe Jack's eye.*)

Jack (*shouts*) Get off! (*He beats his stick on the ground.*) You lot! Listen to me!

Roger We're listening . . .

Jack We're going to do something now. You hear me? Something good.

Roger What's that then?

Jack (*shouts*) Shut up! (*He crosses to Sam 'n' Eric and unties them.*) You two. You new ones. You can serve me if you like. You can come with us. But you have to be loyal. If you're not faithful and loyal then you're punished. You hear me?

Sam We –

Eric Hear –

Sam You.

Jack Bring me that spear. You. Bill. Bring me that spear.

Bill This one?

Jack That one.

Roger What're you going to do with it?

Jack Never you mind. Just listen.

Maurice has been looking over the cliff to where Piggy fell. He turns. He looks white.

Maurice It's miles down there. He fell on the rocks. There's blood coming out of his head, all on to the rock. And his legs are sort of twisted up and broken.

Bill He's as fat as a pig.

Roger Dead pig.

Jack Take this spear. And sharpen it at both ends.

Henry How do we sharpen it?

Jack Rub it. Against the rock.

Henry and Bill get to work. Jack paces.

The beast can move about you see. It changes its shape all the time. But you can tell from a person's eyes if the beast is in them. I know when the beast has got into someone. I can tell by looking at them. I can tell by looking. And when the beast is in someone you have to kill them, like we killed Cambourne. That was all right. It was because the beast was in him. After it was in the . . . fat one, and now it's . . .

Nasty pause.

Roger Where is it, Chief. (*very quiet*) It's not in one of us is it? It's not hanging in the air round . . .

Maurice is still looking down at Piggy's body. Roger moves towards him.

Maurice.

Maurice (*shouts*) Don't!

Roger Just a joke! Just a joke! You laugh at a joke don't you?

Maurice Not your jokes.

Roger Oh you'll laugh at my jokes. And dance to his dance, you will.

Jack It's in Ralph. It's in that stupid stuck up little, weak . . . (*with distaste, as if this was a category that did not include him*) boy.

Roger Hey what's a boy! Anyone seen a boy? I haven't! What's the difference between a boy and a pig? I think –

Jack It's in Ralph and we'll have to hunt Ralph –

Roger Is that a pig . . .

Jack You hear me?

Roger You hear him? Ay ay ayyy!

Jack Ay ay ayyy!

Roger Come on! When the chief says . . . ay ay ayyy . . .

Tribe (*shouts*) Ayyy!

Jack Ay ay ayyy . . .

Tribe (*shouts*) Ayyy!

Jack That's what we do. Whatever we did before with that shell doesn't count. (*Shouts.*) Kill the pig!

Tribe (*likewise*) Spill his blood!

Jack (*again*) Kill the pig!

Tribe (*likewise*) Spill his blood!

Jack (*again*) Ay ay ayyy!

Tribe (*likewise*) Ay ay ayyyy!

> *Jack turns to the forest. Ralph is crouched centre stage, bleeding from the spear blow, out of breath. Perceval, forgotten at the side of the stage, stands like a much younger child, a witness to these horrifyingly adult events.*

Jack You hear that? Wherever you are, Ralph, whatever your name is, you hear? Ralph you hear me? We're coming to get you, Ralph. We can see the beach from the mountain and we'll sweep the forest from here and we'll find you, you hear me? (*pause, then shouts*) Kill the pig!

Tribe (*shouts*) Spill his blood!

Jack (*shouts*) Kill the pig!

Tribe (*shouts*) Spill his blood!

Roger Someone's not shouting!

Jack Someone's not shouting?

Roger Someone's not shouting.

   Pause.

What's a choir if it can't sing? Call that music?

Sam I can't –

Eric Sing I –

Sam Can't.

Roger Kill the pig.

   Eric finds this difficult. But there's a nasty silence.
   Everyone looks at him.

Eric Spill his blood.

Roger Kill the pig!

Eric Spill his . . .

Sam (*shouts*) Spill his blood! Spill his blood!

Roger Good!

Jack (*shouts*) Kill the pig!

Sam 'n' Eric (*together shouting*) Spill his blood!

Jack (*shouts*) Ay ay ayyy!

Tribe (*likewise*) Ay ay ay ayyy!

   Pause.

Jack Let them go.

Roger They might run.

Jack They won't run. (*Close to Sam 'n' Eric.*) Will you?

Perceval steps out of the trees.

Perceval What're you doing?

Pause.

What game is it?

Maurice Over there. Go on.

Perceval There?

Maurice There.

Perceval What's happening?

Roger Never mind. Just move!

And Perceval moves. Now all the group are in a bunch at the top of the stage. Jack steps up to the line of trees, the group moving behind him. They are like one animal now, a beast, compact in its movements.

Jack Hey Ralph! We're coming for you! Can you hear us, Ralph?

Pause.

In a line.

Roger Wait!

Jack Wait for what?

Roger How will we get him in all those trees?

Jack We'li get him.

Roger You think?

Jack I –

Pause.

116

What do you think then?

Roger I think. Smoke him out. (*He takes brands from the fire.*) Work your way through the trees. And when we hear a noise ahead. Set fires. And smoke him out!

The tribe collect brands from the fire.

Ralph is on his way to centre stage, near the pig's skull, looking all round him, still unprotected.

Ralph Please. Somebody. Please.

Upstage, the brands are handed out. The tribe start their chant: 'Ay Ay Ayyy!'

(*He hunches up small*) There can't just be me. There's always . . . there's always someone. When we were at Devonport. Think about Devonport. When we went up on to the moor and there were those . . . what were there, there were . . . (*Hugs himself in fear and misery.*) Simon. And Piggy. Why did they do that to you? How can they?

Jack See anyone? Anyone see anything?

Bill No one.

Henry No one over here.

Maurice No one over here.

Roger I can't see a thing, Boss. I can't see my own dick it's so dark.

Pause.

You! Sam 'n' Eric! See anything?

Sam No –

Eric We –

Sam Don't –

Eric I'm –

Roger has crept over to their side. Pulls one of them viciously by the hair.

What's wrong?

Roger Nothing's wrong. Just checking. You heard what the chief said. Anything you see. You tell. You hear?

Sam I hear . . .

Roger Good . . .

Roger moves them on with a cry. But as they move in a line downstage, Sam, who is in the centre of the line, is grabbed by Ralph. The trees are so thick he can't see and he's about to cry but Ralph stops his mouth.

Ralph Sam –

Sam Ralph . . .

Ralph It's me!

Sam Go away!

Ralph Sam! It's me! It's Ralph!

Sam You must go, Ralph. It's horrible. I can't tell you how horrible . . .

Ralph Where though?

Sam I don't know. Just go.

Ralph Sam –

Sam I'm scared of him. And Roger . . .

Eric Near where the head is there's a run that goes right into the side of the hill . . . you could get in there. And no one could get past. Go deeper into the trees . . .

Perceval I can hear Ralph!

Sam Ralph! Run! Now!

Ralph What's he going to do to me?

Sam Run!

And Ralph runs. A straight run, crouched low like an animal, straight to centre stage where he falls, sobbing for lack of breath, under the pig's skull.

Jack (*shouts*) Where?

Perceval (*shouts*) Here! Talking to Sam!

Jack (*shouts*) Sam!

Sam (*shouts*) I never!

Jack I'm coming over your way . . .

Sam Jack I –

Roger I'll go, Chief. He's nearer . . .

Sam Listen I never . . . I never heard him . . . I never said anything to . . . if I saw him I'd . . .

Roger, to Sam's shock, comes out of the trees behind him.

Roger You'd what?

Sam I'd . . .

Roger You'd what? (*Twists Sam's arm.*)

Sam I'd tell.

Roger You would?

Sam I would. I swear.

Roger You swear?

Sam I swear truly.

Roger is really hurting him, forcing him to his knees.

Perceval I heard them talk.

Sam He didn't. He's a stupid little kid that's all.

Perceval I did. I heard them talk.

Roger Which way did he go? Sammy . . . (*twisting his arm harder.*)

Sam He went . . .

Roger Come on . . .

Sam Please don't . . .

Roger Then tell me . . .

Sam (*shouts*) You're hurting!

Ralph No better than bloody pigs, than . . .

Roger Squeal!

Sam Why are you doing this? Why?

Eric Leave him alone!

Jack (*shouts*) Roger!

> *Ralph has yanked the spear out of the ground so that he has two weapons.*

Ralph Come and get it then! Come and get it if you want to! (*Tosses the skull off and catches it.*) What's the difference eh? What's the bloody difference? (*He dashes the skull to the ground, smashing it with as much fury and viciousness as Roger gave to the shell.*)

> *Over downstage, Roger has forced Sam to confess.*

Sam (*shouts*) Over there!

> *Ralph is forcing himself into the run. A defensive position.*

120

In the bush by the skull.

Jack In the bush by the skull. What skull?

Roger The pig's skull.

Ralph There must be someone . . .

They discover Ralph.

Jack He's talking to himself in there.

Ralph Must be someone who . . .

Jack Must be what?

The tribe are setting their brands to points in a half circle round Ralph. Smoke starts to billow across the stage.

Ralph Must be someone to . . .

Jack There isn't you know, Ralph! There's just you on the whole earth! That's all there is! There's no one else in the whole world! Everyone else is dead and gone! There's just me! And I'm coming to get you!

Ralph There's someone. There is. There always is someone who comes . . . who comes to . . .

This dialogue is softer as they move in for the kill. The figures are getting closer and closer in the smoke.

Roger To what eh?

Ralph To . . .

Roger There may be someone who comes. I don't know. But if they come, they're probably the beast.

Perceval (*shouts*) It's the beast! The beast! The beast!

Sam (*shouts*) Ralph it's the beast!

These screams are as the parachutist figure leaves the trees through the smoke. As he approaches he strips off the makeup that has made him pass for a corpse. All this happens in the thickest part of the smoke, very much as a transformation scene should happen, and before we know it we are looking at the figure of a **Naval Officer** *in whites. Sam is screaming at him.*

(*screams*) It's the beast! Ralph! Ralph! It's the beast!

Ralph is looking out front, as if scared to see what is behind him. The Officer speaks.

Officer Who's in charge here?

Jack starts to step forward.

Ralph I am.

Officer And what's going on?

Ralph It's . . .

Officer What's your name? You. The one in charge. Cat got your tongue?

Ralph My name is . . .

Officer And what's all this about a beast?

Ralph There was a beast and . . .

Officer There was what?

Pause.

A game? Is that it? You all playing a game?

Roger That's right sir. A game. That's all it . . .

Ralph There's two dead. Two of us killed. And the others who . . . (*He starts to cry.*)

Officer Yes?

Roger He doesn't know what he's saying, sir.

Ralph It was all right at first. I kept thinking about my father. He was going to come. But he didn't come . . .

Officer I'll get the others from the boat. We saw your smoke you see. We saw your smoke. (*He still can't quite credit this.*) I should have thought that a pack of British boys – you are all British aren't you? – would have put on a better show than this. Form a line. (*Just before he goes.*) It was a game. Wasn't it? That was all. Eh? (*Pause. He looks at the others.*)

None of them have cracked, apart from Ralph.

Roger Sir.

The Officer goes. The smoke is now clearing. The tribe is still standing round Ralph. Jack, whose face is still blank, steps forward and throws something down before Ralph. Piggy's glasses. Slowly, Ralph picks them up. And, overcome with quite adult grief, he buries his face in his hands as he sits alone, centre stage. There is silence, and one by one the tribe melt away. The final image is of Ralph, alone in the centre of the stage, weeping for the darkness of man's heart and the fall through the air of the true, wise friend called Piggy.

The light fades to blackout.

Property Plot

ACT ONE

Personal:
Piggy: Glasses
Perceval: Satchel

On stage:
Down front, near 'beach':
Creamy white horn-shaped shell (conch) (**Ralph**)
Stone (**Roger**)
All over:
Wood, twigs, branches, leaves, etc., for fire (**All**)
Rocks to contain fire (**Bill, Simon,** others)
Red earth for face paint (**Bill, Jack, Maurice, Roger, Henry**)

ACT TWO

Personal:
Piggy: Glasses
Simon: Blood pouch

On stage:
All over:
Brushwood, branches, sticks, trunks, etc. (**All**)
Large fragment of wood (**Jack**)
Branch (**Bill**)
Trunk (**Sam and Eric**)
Down front, near 'beach':
Conch (**Jack**)
Tattered shelter (**Simon, Ralph, Piggy, Perceval**)
Rocks (**All**)

Sticks (**Ralph** and **Piggy**)
Up right:
Dying fire (**Sam** and **Eric**) In fire: burning brand (**Ralph**)
Wood (**Eric**)
Far left:
Wooden spears (**Jack, Roger, Maurice, Bill, Henry**)
Up left:
Pole for headless carcass of pig (**Hunters**)

Off stage:
Flies:
Parachute (for dead parachutist) (**Stage management**)
Left:
Bloody carcass of pig (**Jack** and **Hunters**)

ACT THREE

Personal:
Piggy: Glasses
Ralph: Blood pouch

On stage:
Down front, near 'beach':
New shelter, deteriorated
Fire with branches, twigs, leaves, etc.
Conch (in shelter) (**Ralph**)
Centre:
Change pig's head to skull
Back:
Change parachutist to skeleton
Far left, up on Jack's 'rock':
Spears (**Jack** and **Hunters**)
Rocks, branches, twigs, leaves, etc. for fire (**Jack, Maurice, Bill**)
Creepers in trees (**Bill, Maurice, Roger**)
Stone to smash conch (**Roger**)

Lighting Plot

ACT ONE

At opening:
Brilliant white light (bright, sunny day), with blue sky effect on cyclorama. (p.1)

CUE 1: **Piggy:** 'You got to do it carefully and prop'ly. You –'
Fire effect at the back of the stage as **Ralph** shouts, 'It's catching.' (p.27)

CUE 2: **Bill:** 'It's spreading!'
Fire effect spreads until the boys control it after they all yell, 'We stamp.' Fire effect continues until end of act. (p.27,29)

CUE 3: **Ralph** looks back almost longingly at the distant sound.
Blackout. (p.42)

ACT TWO

At opening:
Darkness and shadow effect across whole stage with the exception of some light down front near 'beach'.
Moonlight effect. Also dying fire effect up right near **Sam** and **Eric**.(p.43)

CUE 1: **Eric** feeds the fire.
Increase brightness for fire effect. (p.44)

CUE 2: As parachutist falls.
Distant flare effect, like a shooting star. (p.47)

CUE 3: **Simon:** 'If Ralph was here – Ralph would know.'
Faint moonlight catches the pig's head, centre. (p.69)

CUE 4: **Ralph** grabs brand from Sam and Eric's fire.
Burning brand effect for **Ralph**. (p.73)

CUE 5: **Jack, Ralph** and **Roger** notice the parachute.
Faint moonlight effect on parachute; the figure seems to
move.

CUE 6: **Ralph** (*shouts*): 'It moved! It moved! Look at it! It's
alive!'
Lightning flash brings figure eerily to life. More lightning
as the storm breaks. Lightning continues intermittently
until the end of act. (p.74)

CUE 7: **Ralph** puts his brand to the brushwood and sticks.
A fire starts (continues until end of act). (p.75)

CUE 8: **Jack** (*shouts*): 'Hey! Look!'
The fire gets bigger. Quite dramatic. (p.76)

CUE 9: **Simon** picks up a brand from Sam and Eric's fire to
look at the parachutist.
Burning brand effect for **Simon**. (p.80)

CUE 10: **Piggy:** 'Look back the other way. Look at the
island. We ought ter get some sleep.'
Blackout. (p.87)

ACT THREE

At opening:
Brilliant light with blue effect on cyclorama. Fire effect
down front near 'beach'. (p.88)

CUE 1: **Jack** (*shouts*): 'Break up the camp!'
Fire is scattered as **Jack** and his troupe rake through it; fire
dims and eventually goes out. (p.96)

CUE 2: **Jack, Maurice** and **Bill** are crouched over fire up
on Jack's 'rock' with Piggy's glasses.
Start fire effect on Jack's rock; continue until end of play.
(p.103)

CUE 3: **Roger:** 'I think. Smoke him out.'
Burning brand effect for **Roger,** then the rest of the tribe.
(p.117)

Effects Plot

ACT ONE

CUE 1: **Simon:** 'It is . . . it's . . .'
Smoke effect billows from fire, out of control. (p. 28)

CUE 2: **Boys:** 'We stamp!'
Smoke starts to die down. (p.29)

ACT TWO

CUE 1: **Sam:** 'It'll hear us.'
Wind effect for parachute. (p.49)

CUE 2: **Ralph** (*shouts*): 'It moved! It moved! Look at it! It's alive!'
Thunder clap. More thunder, echoing the boys' screams as the storm breaks and they run down the hill. (p.74)

CUE 3: **Ralph:** 'It did move.'
Thunder clap. (p.74)

CUE 4: **All** (*chanting loudly*): 'Kill the pig! Cut his throat! Spill his blood!'
Thunder claps. (p.81)

CUE 5: **Simon** staggers down the mountain, screaming.
Thunder breaks again. (p.81)

CUE 6: As **Simon** reaches the group.
The storm brews and the wind gets stronger. (p.81)

CUE 7: **Simon**, badly wounded, staggers towards the fire.
Wind at its strongest, filling the parachute up on the hill so that the bloody figure seems to lift of its own volition. (p.82)

ACT THREE

CUE 1: **Piggy** falls off the high back of the stage.
Curiously solid sound, like a large weighted sack hitting
the deck. (p.110)

CUE 2: The tribe set their brands to points in a half circle
round **Ralph**.
Smoke starts to billow across the stage. Becomes very
thick to effect parachutist's transformation to **Officer**.
(p.121)

CUE 3: When the **Officer** goes.
Smoke begins to clear. (p.123)